M000223755

million dollar dollar micro business

million dollar micro business

How to turn your expertise into a digital online course

tina tower

WILEY

First published in 2021 by John Wiley & Sons Australia, Ltd
42 McDougall St, Milton Qld 4064

Office also in Melbourne

Typeset in ITC Caslon 224 10.5/14.5pt

© John Wiley & Sons Australia, Ltd 2021

The moral rights of the author have been asserted

ISBN: 978-0-730-39207-1

A catalogue record for this book is available from the National Library of Australia

All rights reserved. Except as permitted under the *Australian Copyright Act 1968* (for example, a fair dealing for the purposes of study, research, criticism or review), no part of this book may be reproduced, stored in a retrieval system, communicated or transmitted in any form or by any means without prior written permission. All inquiries should be made to the publisher at the address above.

Cover design by Wiley
Front Cover Image: © mhatzapa/Shutterstock
Microphone image: © Decorwithme/Shutterstock

Disclaimer
The material in this publication is of the nature of general comment only, and does not represent professional advice. It is not intended to provide specific guidance for particular circumstances and it should not be relied on as the basis for any decision to take action or not take action on any matter which it covers. Readers should obtain professional advice where appropriate, before making any such decision. To the maximum extent permitted by law, the author and publisher disclaim all responsibility and liability to any person, arising directly or indirectly from any person taking or not taking action based on the information in this publication.

SKY0C96BDE4-E8B4-467D-AB19-FC73C54D1AA8_122002722

This book is dedicated to my Empire Builders—the wonderful group of women who dare to dream bigger, who use their talents for good and who inspire me every day to be bolder.

contents

about the author

Starting her first business at the age of 20, an enterprise that went from being a small suburban tutoring centre and educational toy store, to becoming a licence program and then a franchise. After five years of franchising Tina opened 35 Begin Bright centres across Australia that employed 120 staff.

After Begin Bright was acquired by an International education company in 2016, she started coaching other people on how to scale their service-based businesses. When Tina found herself repeating a lot of the same fundamentals again and again to people who were paying top dollar for private coaching, she decided to put the repetitive content into an online course. It went off!

To put location freedom to the test, Tina set off to travel the world for a year with her husband and two children, visiting 28 countries, and all while growing the online business in a couple of hours a day.

Since returning from travel her empire has continued to grow and it's been a revelation to her that this 'little' online business she runs from home, with just a couple of staff, makes far more money and has such a greater and wider impact than her franchise company ever did.

Tina has helped hundreds of people package their expertise into an online course and launch it to the world. Through her program,

Her Empire Builder, she is on a mission to help 100 women build a $1 million a year business by 2025.

Tina is the author of two books, *One Life: How To Have The Life of Your Dreams* and *Million Dollar Micro Business*. Tina has won some cool awards like Telstra National Young Business Woman of the Year Award and Australian Business Champion and has been featured on the *Today Show*, in *the Financial Review*, on Sky Business and as a Business Woman to watch by *The Huffington Post*.

Tina lives with her family on a small farm on the Australian East Coast and from there, helps people to develop and grow their online digital business empires.

acknowledgements

Writing a book is literally the most mentally and emotionally challenging thing that I do. This is only the second time that I've done it and both times have been challenging in their own way. For me, it's the finality of it all! In online courses, I can always re-record if and when something changes, but a book, it's here to stay!

On that note, I want to first thank my family for dealing with the crazy two months before book deadline. That's when I start questioning EVERYTHING and I can be a little difficult to be around and have a conversation that doesn't, in some way, involve this beautiful book. When I told my husband I was writing *Million Dollar Micro Business*, his response was 'Oh my gosh, why would you do that to yourself?' Ha! Well, I do love a challenge, but more than anything, I want to help you to experience the level of success you're after and to design the life of your dreams. So Mat, thanks for doing all of the cooking and for taking care of me so that I could just write.

To my right-hand woman, Jarrah Wallace, how lucky I am to have you in my life! Jarrah is the one who helped to find the facts, pull together our Success Stories and organise my schedule so that I could devote my time to getting all of these many words on the page. There were also many speeches of encouragement and I am so grateful for having your gorgeous support in my corner, Jarrah.

You can guess by reading this book that I'm uber passionate about what I do. The most fun I've ever had in business has been this, right now. Building my program Her Empire Builder and seeing so many women package their expertise, step into their light and share their gifts with the world totally gets me all giddy. I want to thank my beautiful members who have trusted me to guide them and then done the work to elevate their success. You're all kinds of awesome and an inspiration to so many around you.

Thank you to Wiley for pulling this beauty together. In all honesty, most of the work is going to come once the book is sent to print, but I thank you for believing that I could write something worthy of printing and worldwide domination. You guys, when I said 'I want this book to be this decade's *The 4-hour Work Week*' they didn't even laugh at me. Not while I was on the zoom screen anyway ;) Thanks Lucy Raymond, Frankie Tarquinio and Chris Shorten for all of your handwork up to this point.

Thanks to Jem Bates for editing my words and making me sound more witty than I am. If you giggle in this book, chances are it's because Jem tweaked my words to make them funnier and smarter.

I wanted this book to be incredibly useful and not just theoretical. To add some personality and inspiration, I wanted to include some Success Stories from my favourite course creators. It was a little harder than I thought with gate keepers, but I eventually got there! Thank you so much to James Wedmore, Kayse Morris, Clint Salter, Tracy Harris and Denise Duffield-Thomas for so openly sharing your journey and for all of the fabulous work you inject into our world.

Thank you to Kenny Reuter, Jonathon Cronstedt, Allie Fernando and everyone at Kajabi for what you've created and the support that you have provided throughout my course creating and the creation of this book. It's rare that a software company has such personality and customer connection and I love you for it.

Thank you to those who have taught me what I know, some of you I actually know, and some don't even know I exist. It's amazing the incredible people who have helped me through courses, podcasts and content that don't even realise their impact (it's also what I want you to remember when you're creating your content!). Thank you to Amy Porterfield, Jasmine Star, Colin Boyd, Brendon Burchard, Jill Stanton, Jenna Kutcher, Chalene Johnson, Aaron Mac and James Wedmore for all of your gifts to the world that have helped me to figure out and grow in this wonderful world of online digital products.

Above all else, I want to thank you. I wrote this book for you and if you're reading these words, you've picked it up and cracked open the cover. Thank you for taking a punt on this book and thank you for believing in yourself enough to entertain the idea that you can create your own *Million Dollar Micro Business*. It's totally yours for the taking and I'm cheering you on every step of the way.

introduction

That day I sat looking out at the blue ocean spread out before me, reflecting on my past 10 years in business and how much had changed. I was just a couple of months into a round-the-world trip with my family, and we were staying on the island of Ko Lanta in Thailand.

I was having my first proper go at this online course thing I had seen people try. With a background in franchising and a work ethic based on the creed 'while they sleep, I work', I didn't quite believe the hype. And yet, in business I am a curious experimenter. I want to know how things work and the levers to pull to get different results. For this new game, I was still figuring out what the levers actually were.

I had given myself 10 days to write, record and market my new eight-week online course. Of course, it was only possible because I didn't know what I didn't know. Now, having launched courses over and over again, I know the parts I was missing and how 'amateur hour' this first effort was.

But was it actually? In that 10 days in Thailand I had created and sold my course to 11 people. A small number? Yes. But 11 people had purchased a course for $997, or six monthly payments of $199. I knew I was offering spectacular value. I knew they would be able to take the lessons from it and earn back that money multiple times. I also knew that now I had created the course I could sell it many times over. See, putting together an online course is laborious, but once it's done it can be sold again and again and again.

That was when I knew that a million dollar micro business was actually possible. It was the moment I fell in love with this new way of doing business, and knew I would be sharing everything I had learned to help other highly skilled but overworked people to package their expertise and sell it at scale.

I am certain that you have acquired knowledge and skills that are practical and useful, and that you have your own unique spin on them that could help other people acquire the skills and knowledge you have. In this book I want to help you wrap that neatly with a bow into a simple online course so you too can have your moment of staring into space and thinking, 'Holy guacamole, this actually works!'

The way we consume education, like the way we do business, is constantly changing and evolving. Recent technological advances have greatly facilitated the business of online education. Information on any topic you could possibly want to know about is at the tip of your fingers, courtesy of Google and YouTube, but it's often delivered in a disjointed, unmediated flood, like drinking from a fire hydrant. Professionally created online courses provide a linear learning experience that allows the client to define and seek out their desired transformation and access a complete start-to-finish, step-by-step guide. The goal of an online course is to guide a client from where they are to where they want to be in the simplest, most cost-effective and timely way.

I began my further education at university, where I studied Organisational Learning. At the end of my first year I was advised that I wasn't cut out for the corporate world (how right he was!), so I transferred to a degree in primary teaching. I love education. I love learning and teaching, and I knew I had found my calling. Though I have never taught in a classroom, I have been a teacher all my life.

In my second year of studying education I launched my first business, a toy store and tutoring centre on the main street of the suburb where I lived. It was a traditional business in every sense of the word. Business hours were 9 am to 5 pm six days a week and 10 am to 4 pm on Sunday. I employed 17 staff, bought stock from wholesale suppliers, included a mark-up that allowed us to stay competitive, and added value with our custom gift wrapping and branded bags. It was respectable, busy and stressful—all the things expected of a traditional, bricks-and-mortar retail- and service-based mixed business. Four years into it, my first child entered the world.

I went through what a lot of women go through when they have children, beginning with that moment when we realise that the life we had before is no longer going to work for us. I had to figure out how I could operate a business I absolutely loved, maintain my financial independence, satisfy the ambition that burned inside me *and* be the mum I always dreamed of being.

The possibilities for scaling were sparse. Traditional businesses usually see two avenues for growth: work more hours or hire more staff. Neither option was very attractive to me. So I took the curriculum I had created for our tutoring centre and licensed it so other teachers could use it in their own tutoring centres. I then closed my beloved store so I could stay at home with my babies and grow a business around their sleep times. The combination of my love of learning and personal development and my ambition was never going to allow me to keep it slow and steady.

Now, at 37, I have identified a pattern: in everything I do, every plan I make, I seek to escalate, to realise its full potential, and I will help everyone I come into contact with to do the same.

After two years of licensing, I opened our first franchised tutoring centre. I finally experienced the scalability of business!

I imagined I would have franchisees open and operate the centres while I stayed home with my children, a win–win for everyone. But slow and steady was not a game I knew how to play. The business escalated, and in the following four years we opened more than 30 locations. I was working every moment I was awake. I loved the business and dreamed of achieving over 100 locations nationally and operating in multiple other countries around the world. We were already getting proposals for international expansion. On the outside the business looked textbook awesome!

Again, it was a respectable traditional business. When new acquaintances asked what I did, I would say I was the founder and franchisor of a tutoring franchise with 30 national locations (I was still under 30), and they would give me that slow nod with their mouth turned down that said 'Hmmm, impressive'. But it wasn't impressive—it was a yucky way to live a life. The demands were sky high and the expenses even higher. Sure, we had revenue coming in and the business was profitable, but there was always some new improvement I needed to invest in, some giant expense that would swallow up the next allocation of what was supposed to be my financial reward for all the work and sacrifice. I was earning decent money, but I couldn't see how I was going to earn on the scale I wanted in my life without working myself into an early grave.

Although it broke my heart, in 2016 I decided to sell the company I had been building since I was 20, and dare to venture into the unknown—to explore who I wanted to be when I grew up.

Looking back, the six months after I sold my company was a hilarious comedy of errors. I've said that in business I'm a curious experimenter. I'm sure you've been there too, stuck at doing one thing for so long that you've actually forgotten what brings you joy in your work. Or you no longer recognise where your skills and natural gifts lie, because you've had to get good at doing so many other things in your role and now you don't know who you are or what it is you actually want to do with your life …

Sorry, I escalated that a little too quickly! In my case, I opened six new businesses in six months in the hope of discovering what I really wanted to do. Here's how that worked out.

Attempt #1: Shexy

I'm five feet tall, and it's really hard to find clothes made for short women with curves. So Shexy (short and sexy) was born. I sank $40 000 into development before discovering how many, many moving parts there were that would propel me right back into the hectic world of dramatic business before I could blink.

Attempt #2: Jay St

I created a line of jewellery on which inspirational words were engraved. Empowering, yes. Boring? Also, yes. I knocked up a Shopify site in a day, sold my first $5000 worth then sold the business.

Attempt #3: Nikhedonia Productions

This one was the most enjoyable. I was reading a book series to my kids one night and they said, 'Gosh, Mum, I can just see this as a movie'. I had to agree it would make a fabulous movie! Totally Harry Potter meets *Maleficent*, with great messaging throughout. So the next day I contacted the author. A series of meetings and very big contracts later, I had purchased the film rights and set about finding someone to help me produce a movie series. I went to Los Angeles and had meetings with studio executives, and even found myself on a red carpet next to Charlize Theron at a premiere. After many exciting conversations that led exactly nowhere, I realised how very little I knew about the film industry. I simply wasn't willing to risk the next two years of my life on the pursuit of success that was so out of my control.

After that I went back to the drawing board. I read a heap of business books and listened to a lot of podcasts. I was doing some private coaching, as there were a lot of people with service-based businesses who were trying to scale as I had, and I could teach them how to do that. I loved the coaching side of things, so I thought that while I was searching for my next 'real' business I would put some effort into getting better at the coaching craft. I enrolled in a few programs. One of them included an online learning component that allowed me to advance at my own pace. Once I experienced this as a student, I knew I could introduce it into my own programs. All my past experience in business and education meant I was perfectly positioned to write the curriculum in a way that would help people to learn and also to market their knowledge and skills well. That's where the next three businesses came in! I still didn't know what was going to be my thing, so I wanted to test out a few options.

Attempt #4: The Tutoring Institute

This was aimed at helping tutors to grow their tutoring businesses. It was obviously something I knew a lot about, but once I had launched and met with my first few clients I realised that the prospect of doing nothing but talk about tutoring centres over and over again for the next 10 years made me want to retreat into a corner and cry. (Note: Just because you're good at something doesn't mean that's the thing you should be doing. Always go with what sets your heart on fire! Life is too short to stick at something that makes you want to stick skewers into your eyeballs.)

Attempt #5: The Happy Life

I *love* happiness. When I was in my late teens and early twenties, I secretly believed I would grow up and become a motivational speaker! Personal development sets my soul on fire. As I've got older and more worldly wise and worn down by life's demands, I have come to experience more doubts about the idea, even while recognising how much we need it. Positive psychology is something that most of us don't spend nearly enough time on, yet it can greatly enhance our quality of life.

I ran a few in-person happiness workshops, made some gorgeous workbooks and sold the first few people into my program, before recognising that this business was not going to be the winner. While I love happiness and exploring all the things that help create it, I'm a businesswoman who found herself constantly telling people that to be happy they had to start their own business and get out of that job they hate. I love helping people to grow their business and make lots of money and do good things in the world and have more fun. In this I am way too biased to be a happiness guru.

Attempt #6: Scale Up

Ladies and gentlemen, meet our winner. The business that started this online course journey for me. Scale Up was basically what I was doing with business coaching already, but moved from one-on-one coaching to group coaching to many models.

If you've ever hired a private business coach, you know they don't come cheap. This is because their time is their most valuable finite resource. Also, they're usually very experienced, qualified and successful, and you're paying to tap into that knowledge base. But, as I know from my own early experience, you can't always afford a top coach when you're just starting out. Group coaching is a fabulous way both for you as a coach to scale, and also for clients to gain access that they wouldn't otherwise be able to obtain.

$ $ $

Scale Up was initially based on membership. I ran a masterclass each week and a group Q&A session. Private sessions could be added on request.

Through running Scale Up, I found that most of my clients were looking for a way to leverage the knowledge they had in their service-based businesses to be able to help other people and also to create an additional revenue stream. They wanted to be able to create a program like the one they were doing with me, but for their own industry niche. I'm a big believer in giving people what they want. There's an Australian saying: 'Don't push shit uphill'. Running online programs is all about following the path of least resistance by giving people what they want. If your clients are constantly asking you for something, you may want to think about giving it to them.

Now the business had complete location freedom, Mat and I decided to leave everything we knew and travel around the world for a year, sharing some incredible experiences with our kids while they were still young. We visited 28 countries over the following nine months. It was the best year of my life. I could fill a whole book on our adventures, but that's not why you're here. You're here because you know you have a course inside you. You know you've built up some precious skills and knowledge that you can share with the world. And I'm here to show you how.

When I sat there gazing out at the beautiful blue water off that Thai island, I could not believe that I had just made over $10k in 10 days, with barely any expenses, from doing something so easy and so much fun. To make a $10k profit in a traditional business is hard work. And every $10k thereafter compounds that hard work. In an online course business, you do the hard work once, then get paid for it over and over again. I'm unashamed to say that I love earning a lot of money and intend to earn a lot more, because I know what I can do with it. I have seen the impact your money can have.

On our trip I met a girl in Kenya called Annet. She is a remarkable young woman, and although she comes from a poor subsistence village she has very real dreams of becoming a doctor. When I first met Annet and spoke with her teachers and her family, we knew that the only thing that would hold her back was access to education. We made an arrangement to cover her school tuition to a boarding school so she could learn in a safe environment and have her meals and uniforms provided so she could focus on her studies. I promised her that as long as she maintained an A average I would continue to pay for her education all the way until she became a qualified doctor. That was two years ago, and seeing the success that Annet has experienced and how much she is contributing to her local community, we are now granting 16 more scholarships to other girls in the surrounding areas. That's what drives me.

The day I launched my first online course, I took the time to think about what had happened, comparing it with my previous 10 years in business, then looking ahead at future possibilities. It was the biggest revelation of my life. You can do this, I realised. I want this for you too so you can create your own financial independence, help people with your knowledge and make a positive impact in the world.

A million dollar business sounds great, but I've learned on my business journey that not all businesses are created equal. Most people focus on top-line revenue, the total cash money a business generates in a year. In my own businesses, and my coaching career, I have seen many profit-and-loss statements and far too many businesses that may be making a million dollars in revenue, but it's costing them that much or more to run the business. I've seen business owners express pride in their profits, only to admit that when they divide it by the number of hours they work, they're getting around $12 an hour! People were impressed by my franchise company, even though most of the time I earned no more than $50 000 a year—minimum wage.

A traditional business entails hefty running costs, such as staff, rent, equipment and stock. A digital business's running costs can be reduced to little more than a couple of pieces of software. A healthy profit margin for a traditional business will be around 20 per cent, and that percentage doesn't increase all that much as the business grows. In a digital business, profit may begin at around 40 to 60 per cent and as revenue grows so does the profit margin, because the running costs don't grow alongside the business. It's scalable and leveraged—and, my friends, it's beautiful.

A micro business is usually defined as a business that operates on a very small scale with no more than two employees. Earlier I spoke of people's responses when I said I ran a national franchise. Well, the look on people's faces when you explain you have a digital business offering online courses and memberships is very different. The public perception is often still that it's a little side-hustle run from the kitchen table. Let people assume what they want; all that matters is what's important to you.

If you want to run an impressive-looking traditional business that costs you a bucketload to run and gives you stress and pressure in spades, absolutely go for it. The challenge is fabulous and it can teach you so much that will be valuable later. But if it's more important to you to have a business that can make a massive impact on other people's lives as well as giving you a big financial reward and complete location freedom, then a million dollar micro business could be the next adventure for you.

One of my favourite business quotes is 'Revenue is for vanity, profit is for sanity'. I would rather run a million dollar business that makes me $400k a year than a $5 million business making $500k to $1 million a year. It's simpler and a whole lot more achievable to aim for both a great business and a great life. Business owners used to dismiss this as 'too good to be true'; now it's just a different way of running a more leveraged business. Today's technology allows us to do so much more with so much less. Business owners are told constantly that to get ahead they must 'hustle' and work harder than everyone else. But there's a different way of doing things that I didn't truly understand until I launched that course in Thailand. Running a million dollar micro business certainly takes work, but it's very focused and leveraged, so the business can scale while the business owner retains their freedom.

I want to take a moment here to acknowledge that running a digital business still takes work. It won't work unless *you* work. More often than I'd like, I meet people who regard online courses as 'passive income'. By definition, passive income is the product of a set-and-forget investment that more or less effortlessly generates an ongoing profit. Online courses are not passive income, and hearing people sell them as such makes me mad. They also aren't easy. Simple, but not easy.

There's a process to follow to package your expertise into an online program and get your digital business up and running, but, like anything worthwhile, it's going to take much conscious, calculated effort, and you'll need to do things you've never done before. Business is a mind game, and when we approach something for the first time it's often our mental blocks we need to overcome rather than any technical or mechanical challenges. But I've got some great tools that will help you over that pesky hurdle.

Even 10 years ago a digital information business was a relatively complex, and expensive, endeavour. I had a website built for my franchise company less than 10 years ago. I had to get it custom built because the technology to be able to do the things I wanted to do simply wasn't available to us. It was a $50 000 investment. A year after it was built it was already out of date and we needed new software. Now technology can deliver the most wonderful array of options, enabling you to have your idea up and running literally in a day.

I launched my first online program at the beginning of 2018, which isn't that long ago, but even then not everyone was open to learning online. Since then I have witnessed the shift from up close, especially the acceleration through 2020 when the COVID-19 pandemic locked down the world. That brought about not only a broader acceptance of online learning, but also a massive increase in people packaging their skills and expertise into online programs, and customers searching for new things to learn.

There is certainly still a place for traditional educational institutions, but more often now we want to learn something specific to further our life goals, rather than to obtain that precious, overpriced piece of paper at the end of a traditional educational course.

Whether you want to learn how to grow a backyard organic vegetable garden or how to write code for computer programs, you can find a specific course online that will deliver exactly what you need. As consumers, we want quick, easy and economical solutions so we can get on with it. We don't want to sit through an hour-long lecture to glean five minutes of gold; we no longer have the patience to sit through irrelevant content. We are in an age of short attention spans and a world that screams for our attention at every turn. Education has changed to cater for this consumer demand.

Launching an online course business can be a daunting challenge. I wrote this book both as a practical guide to the whole demanding, exhilarating journey and to try to allay the sense of overwhelm that may be holding you back from going for it. You may choose to work through each chapter, implementing each step as you go, but I recommend you do a full power read first, then, with a clearer understanding of the whole process, come back to put into action each step sequentially as you build up your momentum for the big launch.

At the end of each chapter, and throughout chapter 6, the action steps make it nice and easy to check what tasks you need to have completed before progressing to the next stage. Follow these tangible steps and

I guarantee you'll get results. But I don't want this to be just another 'how to' book, so I've folded in some of my own story and experience. To supercharge the inspiration, I've included interviews I conducted on Zoom at the end of 2020 with some outstandingly successful course creators. These role models have been mentors to me as I've progressed on my own online course journey. As you read their stories, you'll soon notice that, rather than following a single, standardised program, each of these remarkable course creators has a different way of doing things. One of the great things about designing your own business is that you get to do it *your way*, the way that best works for you.

I'm a systems girl and love to use good frameworks to make life easier. You, dear reader, can freely access all the beautiful digital resources to support each part of the book at milliondollarmicrobusiness.com. Lastly, a word on terms: You'll find that course participants are variously described as *students*, *clients*, *customers*, even *members*. I use these terms more or less interchangeably. Given that most people I work with are super-qualified professionals, referring to them (accurately enough) as students often sounds wrong. Once they have signed up for a course, I generally think of them as clients.

I recommend you read this book from cover to cover for an overview then use it as a practical handbook, so that by the last page you're well on your way to your first million dollars in online course sales.

I believe everyone has a skill they can package into an online course. You have skills and expertise that other people will want to access for themselves. In sharing your knowledge and skills, teaching others in short, easily digestible lessons, you will embrace the new way of doing business as an online digital course creator and educator. Now let's dive in and I'll show you how.

Part I

How it begins

01
Start small

Often it's not coming up with an idea for your first digital course product that's the challenge; it's choosing just one. People I work with constantly tell me about all the different, sometimes overlapping courses they're going to create. I've shared my first steps already, so you know I started three completely different businesses while trying to discover what I really wanted to do. But I gained traction only when I finally picked just one, starting small and allowing it to grow and evolve.

You've picked up this book, which means you're already interested in online courses and have probably been looking around at them. Maybe you've listened to some podcasts and heard some success stories too. My goal with this book is to persuade you that it's possible to create a million dollar business based on your existing expertise and to show you how to put it all together, ready to launch it out into the world. But I don't want to give you a bum steer. I don't want you to think that when you go live with your gorgeous new website the dollars will come rolling in so thick and fast you won't be able to count them.

Overnight success is possible, but my gosh it's rare. What a digital business does is it allows you to scale and leverage, and it absolutely accelerates your success, enabling you to reach your goals way faster than anything you'll see in a traditional business.

I was talking to someone who runs a course teaching people how to do gorgeous hand lettering. She put everything together in under a month, launched it out into the world ... and got 23 people to buy her product. She was devastated. She'd wanted 100 people for her first course launch. Where that particular goal came from I don't know, but let me tell you, 23 clients for a brand-new online business is something to happy dance about. Once you've started, you can take that experience and build on it.

A digital business gains traction and compounds fast. When you first launch, people who don't buy will at least know about you. Thanks to social media, word spreads rapidly, so, from your first year's performance, if you maintain consistency and keep showing up and adding value for your audience, you'll continue to grow month on month.

If you're looking at how to begin, my advice is to start with what you know. Ask friends and family, 'What do you think I'm best at?' If you're going with what you already know, your credibility in that area is probably already established.

So start small. Your business, like the chapters that follow, won't stay small for long!

02
Personal branding

What follows may trigger some resistance, because if you've never put yourself out into the world before in a big way, man oh man it can be scary! Building a digital business through content marketing and a personal brand is the most effective way to accelerate your growth and reach your goals faster.

'Online' can prompt the misconception that the transaction isn't as personal as shopping in a traditional bricks-and-mortar business. Actually it's more personal. In order to buy from you, your prospective client needs to:

- know you

- like you

- trust you.

You will be able to achieve this *so* much faster if you step forward and own your expertise rather than hiding behind a brand name. If you never want to show your face and be the one talking about your business, then I suggest creating an online course may not be for you.

You may create the most valuable product that the world absolutely needs, but if no one ever sees it, you've totally wasted your time. The way for your products to be seen is for *you* to be seen. It's time to step into the light.

We all feel like we're not good enough in some way. Everyone is unique, but having hang-ups is far from unique. So rather than let it stop you, embrace what makes you uniquely you. This shift in perception can sometimes take time. I know that when I first became a franchisor I had an idea in my head of what a professional woman looked like and decided that was the image I should project. So I marched into Portmans womenswear store and bought a suit and some terribly uncomfortable high heels and practised being more 'professional'. Thankfully, gone are the days when we needed to 'look the part'. That was the old way of doing business. You're now more likely to find the wannabes in designer clothes and the successful ones in jeans and a t-shirt.

A few years ago, after a long day of speaking on stage, I went to the end-of-conference social event to chat with the participants, but soon had to excuse myself and go home. I wasn't overtired or feeling unwell; the problem was my feet were killing me! Trying to look the part meant suffering excruciating pain. I would never show up for an event in flat shoes because I thought it looked disrespectful, and I didn't want the organiser to think I didn't care enough to 'dress up'. But that night I vowed that henceforth I would always wear clothes I was comfortable in. Now I wear an array of gorgeous flat shoes that I can literally bounce around the stage in and have standing conversations for as long as I like! Embracing who you are and what clothes you're comfortable in will always help you perform better. You may *love* high heels—all power to you (and your feet). Just go with what's right for *you*.

The clothes we wear do matter. As a projection of ourselves, they affect how people perceive us when they make that initial snap judgement. We may as well let people judge us on who we really are, because we're going to be judged anyway. I love colourful clothes and wearable art.

I'm sure some people will see me and think I look like a ridiculous walking rainbow, but others will think how wonderfully colourful and happy I look. Attract (or polarise) your audience by showing up as you really are. You'll be much happier for it, because your clients will be people who are attracted to the same vibe.

Having a personal brand doesn't mean having no privacy. This is one of the most common objections I hear. When we think of personal brands, we may think of Instagram influencers flooding the world with selfies and model poses. By 'personal brand', I mean showing up as yourself, allowing the world to see the massive value you offer, and not dimming your light.

Decide now, as you embark on building your personal brand, what parts of your life you're happy to share and what parts you'd prefer to keep private. What works for someone else might not work for you. It's up to you to decide how much of yourself you want the world to see. Back in 2016 I had to deal with a cyber stalker. The experience totally shifted my relationship with the internet, social media and how much of my life I shared. I am very open and will share pretty much everything about my business and happily answer anyone's questions. I make myself readily available online to talk about business and some of my hobbies. I have two children but they're rarely in my social media. You won't find a tour of the inside of my house, or where I'm on holiday until I've left the location, and you'll very rarely see me sharing my experiences with friends or family. My social media is for business and I am very purposeful about that. People buy my expertise, and they need to know I have credibility in that area before they do, but at no point in our transaction do they buy *me*. Building a personal brand does not mean you need to show your personal life. It means you can decide which parts you're happy to share so your clients can get to know you, leaving everything else for your wonderful private life.

For example, I show all around my office; my dog frequents my account because she's always at my feet; I share what I'm working on and what roadblocks I come up against so I can also share how I overcome them. I share my goals and sorrows where they relate to business, but not the rest of my life. Your clients don't care about that. They care about how you can fix the problem they're trying to solve and how equipped you are to do that.

I've talked about the merits of starting small and starting with one thing. This is easier not only for you but for others too. If family, friends and colleagues want to recommend you, you want to make it as easy as possible for them to do so. This means understanding exactly what it is you do and who you do it for, so you need to communicate clearly and explicitly who you serve and what you stand for.

When people speak about you when you're not in the room, what will they say? The personal brand you've crafted and projected—that's what will do the talking for you.

03
Time management

Perhaps the seed to start your own online course was planted long ago, or maybe it's a new idea. Either way most likely you're not someone with a surfeit of time and no idea how to use it.

'I'd love to do this. I just don't have the time' is the number one objection I hear. In reality, you have time for everything that's most important to you. We're all time poor because we humans always want to do more than the time we have available, so we find ourselves in this perpetual cycle of disappointment, running faster and faster as we try to do everything, yet our goals keep eluding us.

To master time you need to spend it doing the things that bring you the most joy and the most money, and either outsource, automate or simply eliminate the rest. I talk a lot about this in my book *One Life: How to Have the Life of Your Dreams*, where I recommend a structure to time audit your life. Many of us fall into the trap of spending far too much time on the things that don't matter and not enough time on the things that do.

Spending time on packaging your knowledge and expertise and creating an online course is such a good use of your time. It will help other people with what they seek to learn, while also returning a financial reward and helping create a legacy for you. But it's not enough that I believe it for you. You have to believe it yourself so you prioritise this work and get it done. And when you hit the mental roadblocks, your belief must be strong enough to help you push through beyond your comfort zone because you know it's worth it. If it's not worth it to you, then you'll never have time for it, because something more important will always come up. Your most important value will always hijack your time.

Overthinking

Hello there, my overthinkers and perfectionists. Yes, you need to put great thought into what you're going to do and how you're going to do it, but there's a line beyond which you have to say f*#k it and just go and do it. No more thinking. Time for action.

At the beginning of this year, clients of mine finally launched their first six-week course. They'd been planning it for over a year. About six months before they launched it was clearly ready, but there was always something else that needed to be revisited, a delay on getting filming done or a worksheet that should be revised. When they launched, they had students join their program from their first webinar, and they were understandably ecstatic. That win gave them confidence to go on and relaunch. They grew quickly, and now they're racing ahead with their online programs and building a healthy revenue stream.

That money could have been flowing in six months earlier, though. Now, when it comes to creating new content for their courses, they find the time and get it done because they know they can do it and they know it's going to yield a positive result. I want you to know that now. Take action and launch. Don't waste months—in some cases, years—while finding excuses not to take the action that's going to deliver the result you want.

Finding time

It's not all mind games, of course. There's still the very real barrier of the massive commitments you have in your life already and the challenge of how you can practically carve out the time to pursue this new adventure. You will find you can get it done in a limited time. You just need to choose your path of stolen moments. I'm a batching fan. In fact, to write this book I took myself off to a far-away place and set myself up alone with no distractions so I could focus solely on the writing. It works better and faster for me if I can get into the right frame of mind and go all in, which is why I record my courses in one hit. I put myself in that zone and I go for it. I may feel tired, self-doubt, scared, even bored, but I am committed to the end result, which is so much more important to me than any mood that washes over me while I'm working on it.

The alternative is stolen moments, which may be your only option if you can't or don't want to bail on normal life for a week. This means carving out small, batched moments when you can be super purposeful with your time. If this is real for you, if you're determined to get this done, you need to allocate at least 30 to 50 hours to getting your first online course and business ready for the world.

Grab your calendar and block out the time now, whether it's a full week or a four-hour block every Tuesday afternoon for the next few months. Put it in your calendar and then protect those times. Don't let anything get in the way. Treat the time with as much respect as you would an appointment with your child's orthodontist with a non-refundable appointment fee.

Later I'll show you what to do to ensure that the time you spend is purposeful and conscious and gives you the maximum return. There's no space here for procrastination. In this limited time you must get in and get a result. Then, in a few months' time, you'll have your prize, a fully launched online program.

You have to be conscious and committed in how you spend your time, or your whole life will end up being filled with the unimportant.

Every time you make a time decision, you're reinforcing what's most important to you. Every time you say yes to something, you unconsciously say no to something else. You can do absolutely anything, but not everything. What can you say no to in order to free up the time to create something epic? If you want to achieve your goal, you have to sacrifice the time needed to put in the work and make it happen. It's not like a traditional business, where your goal may take years and years of slogging away, and bucketloads of cash to fund. Stop overthinking it and take bold action now in pursuit of your dreams.

04
Overcome your fear

Before you even begin creating an online business, you have to overcome your fear. You can read this book and run through all the technical 'how to' steps to get you started, but more than anything business is a mind game. And online business differs significantly from traditional business in that you are putting yourself out there at the front. There's no brand to hide behind. It's you, your expertise, your thought leadership.

You're streaming live online, sharing your thoughts and ideas around making a positive impact in the world. It's great, but there's no getting around it—it's scary. It's very easy to fall into the comparison trap and not feel good enough, to be so concerned with the judgement of others that you feel paralysed, afraid to step into the light and share your gifts with the world. Fear is the number one barrier that holds people back from achieving their dreams.

You're reading this book because you're attracted by the vision of building a million dollar business with a few staff, and making a big impact in the world, while still having the space and time to live a great life outside your career. All the tools you'll need are available to you, but you have to want that vision badly enough that your desire outweighs the fear you'll inevitably feel when you push through beyond your comfort zone to do things that you've never done before.

One of the best solutions to overcoming fear that I have learned is what Tim Ferriss calls *fear setting*. The link to his original TED talk is at milliondollarmicrobusiness.com.

Here's a simplified version:

1. Fill in the table that follows with everything you're afraid of

When you think about creating your course and sending it out into the world, what is it you're afraid of? For example, you're spending all this money on getting the business started. What if it doesn't work? What's going to happen in the world down the line? What if you put it out there and everyone thinks, 'She doesn't know what she's talking about'? What if you put it out there and nobody buys it? Write down every single fear you have. Go to town—include them all!

2. Out of all those fears, what is the absolute worst thing that could happen?

I want you to go all doomsday here! Let your imagination run wild. Next to each of those fears, write down the absolute worst-case scenario for what you think could happen.

3. How would you recover from the worst-case scenario?

Imagine it has actually happened. In reality, the odds of every fear coming true are very, very slim and the potential upside is way more likely than the potential downside, but just in case the very worst should occur, and every single fear comes true, think about what it would take for you to recover from that to be exactly where you are right now. You'll find that often even the worst-case scenario is not that bad, and is certainly not enough to stop you from chasing your dreams and stepping into your new online business.

Whenever I feel like fear is holding me back from doing something, I think of the absolute worst-case scenario. My fears might go something like:

What if nobody buys my new program?

What if people think I'm an idiot?

What if I waste all of my money?

What if I waste my time?

Then I look at how long it would take me to get back to where I was at the start. Usually after a failed business experiment it takes a month or two to recover and return to normal. I think I'll take that risk.

Let me tell you, all business is an experiment, whether you're new to the game or have decades of experience. You may look at people who seem to model your version of success and imagine they have never taken a misstep, but that just doesn't happen. We never cease to evolve and learn and take risks. A successful business is a beautiful experiment where you either win or learn.

So work out the absolute worst-case scenario if you were to go ahead. Could you deal with that situation? When you get comfortable with the worst-case scenarios and know how you'll recover from them, you are absolutely unstoppable.

4. What's the potential upside?

This is the fun part! You allowed your brain to do the catastrophising; now imagine what it would be like if it all turned out to be easy. What would it be like if all your dreams came true? What would life actually look like for you if you made seven figures a year, had a small, loyal team and did meaningful work that matters? It's a beautiful feeling when you prove to yourself that you can do something you've only ever dreamed of. If you're committed, it's not a matter of *if* but of *when*, and how many lessons you'll need to learn from failed experiments before you get there!

A fear-setting exercise

What I want to do:

Potential downside (my fears)	What would happen if those fears came true?	How would I recover?

Potential upside (my dreams)	What would it mean for my life if it came true?

It's totally natural to feel nervous and apprehensive at the beginning of an exciting new journey. Of course you don't know what you're doing—you've never done it before. The only way to figure it out is to actually do it. Keep reading, and I'll show you how.

Action step

Complete the fear-setting exercise.

SUCCESS STORY

James Wedmore
Business By Design

James Wedmore was born and raised in sunny Laguna Beach, California, and now lives and runs his business in the beautiful Red Rocks country of Sedona, Arizona. For the past 15 years James has leveraged his expertise to help teach digital CEOs how to build and scale their online businesses through courses and training, such as his signature program, Business By Design. Other programs in James's abundant course library include Sales Page By Design and Nail Your Niche.

Celebrated in the online space for his unrivalled online courses and content, James also facilitates Next Level, a strategic, group-coaching experience, and the high-level mastermind The Inner Circle.

When he isn't working, James can be found hiking, flipping homes for Airbnb, or off-roading through the rocky terrain of Sedona. His motto is simple: 'Work hard, play harder!'

We had the following conversation in September 2020.

Can you give me your origin story?

Well, I have like 20 origin stories.

The one I know is you went into video then pivoted into online courses.

I call it the leapfrog effect. I think everything you're going through now is just preparing you for the next thing. So there's an origin story for every next thing. But the story of how I stumbled across this idea of selling teaching information, coaching on the internet, started when I was bartending at a restaurant, on the day shift during the week, which is kind of depressing, while on the weekends I was running a mobile bartending business where people hired me to come to their parties. I wasn't passionate at all about bartending. I don't even drink more than a glass of wine once a week. But I was passionate about business. So within a year I had this mobile bartending business with 15 staff members and we were servicing parties north of LA all the way down to San Diego, so a big chunk of Southern California. We were booked solid every week, while I was consuming book after book and program after program on how to understand running a business and marketing. And I noticed a pattern. Everyone I was learning from was selling their system on marketing and business — that was in November of 2007, so you can see how long ago it was — and I had the idea that I could do the same. It kind of started as a game for me. I thought, I bet I can make more money teaching people how to tend bar than actually doing it. That night I came up with the domain name Bartend For Profit, and my idea for an online bartending school was born.

I moved back in with my parents and buried myself in my room. I put all my marbles into this jar of creating an online bartending website and business. It was April 2008. Several months later I had a finished book (220 pages) and a CD-ROM with video training and all that stuff. And, bada bing, bada boom, I had my very first sale. That was, you know, one of the greatest moments of my life. A complete stranger from San Antonio, Texas, paid me $200 plus $19.95 shipping and handling to send this entire at-home and online package — I did both, so you got a print version and a digital version of my bartending thing. I knew even back then I wasn't going to stay with bartending, I wasn't going to be the bartending guru, but that one day this would turn into something bigger and better.

Do you think your initial success was partly because you started with what you knew at the time?

Yeah, I had to start with what I knew. I also had to have a vision of where I could go, and, you know, that's the thing that people don't get, and I'm just very lucky that I did get this. But if your heart isn't in it, you're not going to be successful. It's very easy for people to see what I do today and see the money I make, the lifestyle and, you know, the fame, the huge following, and they want all those things. But they don't understand that that's a by-product of the work. They fixate on the by-product and not the work. What happened was I fell in love with marketing, I fell in love with technology, copywriting and selling. I fell in love with teaching too. If people fall in love with money and freedom and significance and influence, they're chasing the wrong thing. I hear people all the time say, 'I just don't like marketing' or 'I don't like writing' or 'I don't like the internet'. And it's, like, then what are you doing? My secret is I love what I do. I love all of it.

From bartending, how did you then get into the video program? Because the video program was really what took off for you, wasn't it?

Someone who saw what I was doing connected with me and asked, 'Will you partner with me in my business?' He was a dating and relationships coach. This was maybe the end of 2009. He just wanted to be the relationship coach. I said, great, let me do everything else. At the time he had a $37 ebook that was making like a sale a week. So he was making 150 bucks a month. I said, move over and let me do it. And I went to work. We completely reinvented his marketing strategy. Within the first month, we were already on track to build a six-figure business. There were no ads at the time, none of this stuff we have today.

So practically overnight he went from $2000-plus a year to a six-figure business, and growing. Every month was bigger and bigger. One of the big things I did was I took a YouTube channel of his from zero to two million views in about two months. That's how we built the business.

Then one day he calls me up. I was getting a percentage. He said, 'Well, looks like the business is working now'. And I said, 'Yeah, sure is'. He said, 'So I don't need you anymore'. And he let me go.

I was really green at the time. I thought we were partners. I thought this was *ours*, that I had a 30 per cent stake. But no, I was just an employee. Because he didn't have money then, he was just going to pay with the revenue. But we didn't have any contract in place, so he just fires me one day, and it's back to square one. I'd dropped everything else and for the last year had focused 100 per cent on that business. And there I was just, you know, dumped, and no more money coming in.

By the relationship coach!

Yes, by the relationship coach. I know, there's the subtle humour. He dumped me and I was upset, angry. I was even scared ... for two steps. I walk or pace while I talk, so I took two steps, then on the third I told myself, I'm going to decide that this is *the best thing that ever happened to me*. This is a true story, exactly how it happened, I could take you to the spot in the middle of the street in my neighbourhood where I made that decision.

I got off that call and made my decision. Life is a choice, so everything that happens is about the decisions we make. What am I going to make out of this? Two weeks later, a friend came and crashed on my couch for a week. Lewis Howes was kind of my peer and became a really close friend. We'd been learning and struggling together. And he started telling me how frustrated he was by people who were letting him down, being dishonest and doing shady things. I'm going through exactly the same experience so I say, 'I know what you mean'. And he tells me, 'From now on, I only want to do business with my friends'. I'm sitting there and I say, 'Yeah, me too'. He looks at me and he goes, 'We should do something'. And I say, 'Yeah, we should'. And he goes, 'Let's create an online course'. And I say, 'Yeah, that sounds great'. And he goes, 'What do you want it to be about?' And I say, 'Well, I just helped this guy get millions of views on YouTube. How about YouTube?'

I had a film background too, so I knew how to make videos, but I was really into how to use YouTube. This was in January 2010. Right after this guy had dumped me. And he said, 'Okay, let's make a product on YouTube'. So I created it, and we launched it in September 2011 and made a good $400000 in sales in 30 days at a $97 price point. Overnight I became the YouTube guy. That product went on to do a couple of million dollars in sales. And it spawned an entire business.

How did you even do that? Facebook, which you used to promote your products, had just started then.

Yeah, the way we did it was with a very simple model that you don't see a lot of people use today. My superpower, especially at the time, was teaching. I was just really good at teaching and making things simple and fun and easy to do. Lewis didn't really like teaching, but he was a super connector, which at the time I wasn't at all. He had all these powerful, influential friends and himself had a big audience. So he put me in front of his audience and then he started attracting these people as affiliates.

So you came right out of the gate with your first course with affiliates and the whole shebang.

Yeah. We used affiliates and joint-venture webinars and stuff like that. And we were doing three a day, I was finishing one and jumping straight onto the next. We used GoToWebinar and sent people to a checkout page. And that was it. It was still really simple. And it was amazing. Then I built several other products and coaching programs.

Was that week as exciting as when that guy in San Antonio bought the first bartending product?

That's a great question. They were just very different. The first one told me, this really is possible and you can do this. This one told me, you can live an extraordinary life and reach the top doing this. One was I can do this, the other showed me what was really possible when I did. So both were very exciting. But I think it's still more exciting to discover it's possible, because it wasn't always about the money. Money was one driver, but only to the extent that I didn't want to have to worry about getting a job.

Now you make millions, is the same level of excitement there?

You can see yourself getting desensitised. I think you can choose to hold on to as much gratitude and appreciation as possible. One of the things I talk about with my students and help my students with is what we call Launch Freefall. You've put all this time and effort into creating this program and everything around it, then you put it out there and it doesn't go the way you expected. The only expectation you should have is that it won't go the way you expected—that I can guarantee! So I'm desensitised to the ups and downs of the Launch Freefall. Everything is just always okay.

We do big launches today, $6 million launches with 150 affiliates and a team of 12. We're doing long days and 50 000 people are going through the launch. Things happen. Today I'm cool as a cucumber. It's just whatever, you know, it is what it is. I think that's just a beautiful place to find yourself—never being reactive or freaking out and emotionally all over the place. Because the way I look at a launch is it's like a Broadway stage performance. If you're too much in your head, or you're freaking out, you're affecting the performance and if you're affecting the performance, you're affecting sales. So every time I go into a launch I simply ask myself, what does my audience need from me today?

When you keep creating new goals, there's that excitement at every launch. Once you get past a place of *is this possible?* and *can I do it?* the only thing that really lasts, that will drive you over the long term, that isn't like a drug where the high wears off, is to find yourself in a place where the core motivator is service and impact. I know that sounds like a cliché. But when someone comes to you and says, I was on food stamps and now I just bought a home and my spouse has retired, because of what I've learned from you ... well, that's a high that never wears off. It's something you can never get sick of. And that's all we do today, because I'm all about the long term. You'll always notice

that about me—I don't follo
current, because trends come a
I have is rare and becoming rare
strategy. That's kind of one of my s

If you want to do something long term, t
pulls you long term. Money won't do tha
money is one of the weakest motivators. C
then it doesn't drive them the same way. That
We took our company from $3 million to $9.4
told people I was going to do that, and they laughe
easy, it was so easy to do that. But I'll tell you this.
for me in terms of my lifestyle, my quality of life, my
Nothing at all changed there. It doesn't get any better.

As your skills grow, so will your rewards. One year I quadruple
revenue on my own—without any partnerships, and not worki
Lewis—and took the business from about $280 000 to $1.2 m
in revenue. That's a quantum leap in growth. People generally exp
like 10 per cent a year, a little step. This is a rite of passage if you're
personal brand, influencer or course creator. People ask me, what was
my secret? What did you do to quadruple your revenue in one year?
Was it a new launch strategy? Was it more Facebook ads? It was one
thing: I finally let go of the need to be liked.

So many people come into this industry and see everything through
the lens of I hope they'll like me, I hope I say the right things, I hope
I get engagement, I hope they give me compliments. People have no
idea how little I care about others' opinions of me. Even when someone
says something nasty or bad, it's oil and water. It has zero effect on me.

**How did you get to that level? I find that's what holds so many
people back—when they go to launch and they're so worried about
people's perceptions.**

Well, for starters, you have to realise it requires a deep inquiry into
your own life—you know, how much your life is being dimmed and

ɔroval and good

alone. Even if

wn to you and

ᴇ. No one else

ı very short

ɔr what am

dgements

ging you

fraid of

ıt they

ɔn your

to be.

ʲith your

ᴜ.tent — had been

_ ᴛo *get them to like me?* I

_ ɑnd double second-guess it. I was

..ıor on it. A governor is a term used by auto

..vıce that throttles back the carburettor so it doesn't

ᴜore and burn out the engine. I was holding myself back from

ᵍ.ıng pedal to the metal in my messaging and even my self-promotion. Oh, I don't want to come across as pushy, because then they won't like me. So I don't say anything. When none of that matters you open the floodgates and you're just unapologetically you.

Here's my thing. I don't care if you don't like it. If you like it, great — here's what to do. If you don't, that's great too. What that does is it encourages you to amplify your message, which becomes more powerful and reaches far more people.

So what shifted in the business? This is where people get all screwed up. And this is why I teach goal setting today, which is really fun because I have a whole different approach on goal setting. The goal should be to fulfil your purpose or dharma every day. Mine is to transform and empower change makers and entrepreneurs to be the best versions of themselves so they can reach more people. That's the goal, and I pursue it every day in some capacity, whether it's through a new podcast episode or a coaching call with my clients. Every single day someone says this helped me, thank you. So I focus on the goal every day, but the game is in the way I'm going to do that.

My goal hasn't changed for years, but the game changes all the time. That's a big, big distinction that most people don't get. They focus on money as the goal, and when they don't hit the money, they get upset. Look at me, I'm a failure—self-pity, self-pity. The reality is that goal you created is outside of your control, because you don't have control over the thoughts, habits, actions and behaviour of complete strangers on the internet. You can influence them but not control them. You've said, I'm going to make my identity, my beliefs about myself and my emotional state completely dependent on an external variable I have no control over. How is that working out for you? Instead, my goal is to do something I do have control over, which is to be of service or to put something out there that's going to help at least one other person. I can say and do that every day. And if I'm doing that, then I'm already winning.

For people looking to get their gifts out into the world, do you think it's harder now because the space is more crowded?

Well, it depends on what you mean by 'harder'. The simple answer is yes, but let me make a key distinction. When there are more people doing what you do, you may complain that the market is overcrowded or oversaturated. This is a belief that is rooted in lack, and lack is an illusion. That's a hard idea for people to take in. I operate from a context that lack is an illusion. There's no such thing as lack. You don't believe me? Go look in nature. My home borders on national forests. Thousands and thousands of trees, and thousands of leaves on each one. How many grains of dirt and sand cover this beautiful desert of Sedona? Abundance is everywhere. You make a choice when you see lack rather than abundance. So I don't look at market saturation; I look at market sophistication. It's not that there are too many people; it's that the market becomes more sophisticated, and you need to become more sophisticated than the market.

So it's hard only in the sense that your skills as a communicator, an influencer, a marketer and a copywriter need to match the sophistication of the current market. If you're trailing the market, you're losing. It's not until you get ahead and lead the market that you win. Today, with what I know and what I've done, that's very easy for me to do. But for someone without the necessary marketing skills, yeah, it's going to be hard for them. Because it's like trying to be the best architect when you didn't go to architecture school, right?

How do you view social media marketing with your personal brand?

The first thing I would say is when I'm creating content about my life, it's never from a place of *what do I want to share?* or *what will persuade people to like me?* but rather, *what about my life will provide value for somebody else?* That's the difference. You know, I think there are chronic over-sharers. And they're doing so out of a need for significance and attention, a need to be liked, which we've already talked about. None of that matters to me. Why do I need attention? Okay, that's just completely irrelevant to me. What I want is to help people, and if this helps them, then I want it in front of them so it can help them, and if it can help more people, I want to get it out in front of more people. So everything I do passes through that simple lens. To me, it's as simple as that.

How did your habits change from when you reached that first million?

My answer to this might be a little different from most people's. When I hit that $400 000, I fell into a deep depression, and I'm normally a pretty happy, easygoing dude. I just started drinking and smoking pot and couldn't get off the couch. The reason for that, as I found in hindsight—because hindsight is 2020—is that I had tied my sense of self-worth to some elusive dollar amount in the bank account. If I make a certain amount of money, then I will be good enough, I will be worthy enough, girls will want to date me, friends will want to like me, people will want to love me. And when all that money came in, I didn't feel any different. I was the same insecure loser I saw myself as. And that was very scary, very confronting. What got me out of it really was that I went down a path of spirituality. I developed a spiritual context in my life, and it changed everything. This is why I talk about this so much, because it changed my life and I want to give back. If what I have, and what I've done, resonates with you and you'd like to learn a little more, here's what I discovered in my own life.

The first thing that had to go was this strategy that most of us have, which is that in some way we've equated our work ethic and our effort with our deservedness. If I work enough, if I work harder, then I will be deserving of success. I decided I never ever wanted that to be the case. So what I tell my students today is, you should never work hard to be deserving of what you want. Work hard, because your clients deserve the best. They deserve the best of you. But it has nothing to do with your being more deserving.

And I can say that, conceptually, everyone is going to have to go on their own journey to work through that. Because the scariest thing is to spend years of your life working harder and longer only to wake up and realise you still tell yourself that story. I'm not worthy enough, and no amount of work will ever change that. Trust me. When you can be at peace with who you are, with the idea that you are worthy, that you are deserving; then you're not working from a place of fear or compensation, you know, trying to compensate for a lack. Everything you do is because you put your heart into it. So I want the people who come into my world to experience my best stuff. Because they deserve it. That's it. I pour my heart into everything I do because I love it and it doesn't feel like work.

How much do you work now in terms of effort? Do you quantify work now?

I hesitate to answer because the way the business runs is in cycles. It ebbs and flows. This year especially is very different, because last year there were 21 events. I had two masterminds with three events each.

So there's six events right there. Then I had a program called Business By Design, then Next Level, and that came with two events. So now we're at eight. Then we ran two BBD lives a year. So there's 10. And I ran an affiliate mastermind for people who had won one of our big competitions.

What is the first thing you think someone should do when they're starting in the online course world?

The first thing they should do is sell it. People waste too much time in their comfort zone. The proof is in the pudding, as they say, and the pudding is the profit. You don't have a business until someone gives you money. So why not be in business? Now, instead of spending a year working for free trying to build something, the reality is, you don't need all that stuff.

You get started, you can just sit there and say, I want to help people do this. And if you'd like me to teach you, here's how to sign up. We've had people do their beta launch or founding members launch with just two people. Better two than none. The problem is, it's as simple as this. Ours is a unique type of business. I mean, I've seen people who have been in other businesses come into this industry and get their butts kicked. And part of it is because their identity is wrapped up in the product, you know, and all they get to deal with is these confronting issues around themselves.

The other part of it is, well, kind of tied up in that. It's the Pareto principle on steroids—*5 per cent of the activities you do are directly responsible for 95 per cent of the results you want*. The problem is, that 5 per cent is often far outside people's comfort zone. They can stay busy and distracted for a long, long time. What I like to say is business is very seductive and it will trap you all the time. Oh, I've got to do this first. But I need to do that first. I need to do my photo shoot and my business card and my website. I need to podcast, to get the Instagram, to produce six months of content. Now I need to do that. And a year goes by and they're like, 'I don't get it. I've been working my arse off and have nothing to show for it'. That's because *the only things that will drive the business forward exist way outside your comfort zone.* And what is that at its core? It's making an offer, asking people for money, selling. Maybe I can do this without selling. But you can't. You have to sell. You have to ask for money. And if you don't ask for money, no one's gonna give it to you.

Anything you would like to add for course creators?

There's a lot happening on the planet. I stand in a place where it's all good. And I think it will just bring more awareness and enlightenment and beautiful things to us. It's just like all the personal growth I've had to do in my life. I had to go through some crap to do it. And that's what anyone who's done any type of internal work will tell you. It's tough because you've got to face the parts of you that you don't want to look at, and you've got to deal with them. Then, on the other side, it's beautiful. And I believe we're doing this collectively, whether we want to or not, and that's beautiful.

Part II
Create that first idea

05
Get clear on your idea

The first thing you'll want to do is all the fun stuff, such as coming up with your business name, your branding, your course, filming and all the action-taking things. But the first thing you *should* do is get really clear on your idea.

Clarity is the key, so you don't sprint a million miles in the wrong direction or, worse, in all directions. I want to save you time and money by helping you to get clear on your idea before we dive into the technical aspects. This chapter is about nailing a really clear, concise, well-thought-out idea, ensuring you have heaps of clarity around your target market, what you're trying to build, why you're trying to build it and what you're going for.

You have an incredible opportunity. Never in history has there been a better time to start your own business. The amazing, unprecedented access to technology and knowledge we enjoy makes getting a business started really quite affordable.

You can complete the entire process and start your business on less than $5000. Ten years ago that wasn't even possible. Today the software is affordable and simple to use and the marketing avenues are established and available to everyone. Gone are the days when spending a small fortune on a fancy custom website and branding and advertising were needed to launch. The tools for creating an online course business are readily accessible to all. You can teach and talk about what you love, enriching the lives of so many people while at the same time enriching your own life.

In this part of the book there are loads of interactive exercises to help you get really clear on your idea, so you can use it like a workbook. Alternatively, if you want to do it digitally, head to milliondollarmicrobusiness.com to download all the resources.

Brainstorming

First let's talk about the difference between easy and effortless. We want to design your business around something you find effortless. That doesn't necessarily mean it's easy; rather, it means it's something you love to do, which (if you haven't already nailed it) is what we're going to figure out as we go through this process. You probably already have a pretty good idea in the back of your mind of what you want to do, which is great. But before we go full steam ahead we should make sure it's the perfect idea.

The first thing to look at is what you're good at, which may not be what you're actually trained in. Sometimes what you're good at isn't what you really enjoy either, so that isn't going to be a winner. We need to find the winning combo for you. This means taking a look at your history and the skill set you've built over time.

For myself, I've got a lot of business experience, having built and sold businesses in retail, licensing, franchising and online, managed large teams, navigated legal issues and all points in between, all of which has left me with a beautiful, solid business knowledge bank. I'm a qualified primary school teacher. I have a knack for breaking complex things down into simple steps. And I'm really good at getting things done—that's pretty much my superpower. The combination of these strengths allows me to do the business and live the life I do.

Think of the different combinations of things you're good at. Dealing with children? Being seriously organised? Great at marketing? What are the things you're really good at? Write them all down so we can figure out the common thread that will allow us to combine them. This isn't the time to be modest! Recognise the expertise and skills you've acquired over your life and just brain dump them down.

What I'm good at:

_____

_____

_____

_____

Next, think about what you could talk about all day long. Believe me, once you've designed your online course, you're going to be thinking and talking about it constantly! You'll dream about it and wake up thinking about it. It will permeate your life.

What's more, it will be what people associate with you when they talk about you. You'll be asked questions about it all the time. This is why you have to love it. If you do something that you're good at and that will make money, but you don't wholeheartedly believe in it, you won't enjoy long-term success, and you'll most likely be miserable. My main motivation for sharing everything with you in this book is to help you create a business that brings you and your clients joy.

So you need to be able to, and to want to, talk about it all day long. I have a friend who's a doctor and he hates it. So at parties he never says he's a doctor because he doesn't want people to ask him about it. That's not what we want for you. Imagine, you meet someone at a party who says, 'Oh my gosh, I saw you put together a course on organic gardening. How can I start this at my place?' And you say, 'Yay! Let me tell you all about it'. It's your thing, and you are happy to talk about it all day long, which is just as well because you'll be running lives on social media and your own podcast and getting interviewed on other people's podcasts, where you'll be asked the same questions again and again so you just can't get bored with it. You have to believe in the message and want to serve.

Of the things I'm good at, what could I happily talk about all day long?

What is it that people naturally ask you about? What do they know you for? It may not be obvious. If people are asking you about something because they've observed that you're really good at and knowledgeable about it, that's a pretty good indication that you've already started building your knowledge, expertise and credibility in that area. Think about what people already ask you about, assuming your superior knowledge or skill. What can you do easily that others find challenging?

Let me give you a personal example. So much of what I do is second nature to me. When someone asks me how to do something, I find it's usually something I don't even consciously think about—I just naturally get it done. Yet identifying these areas can be challenging, which is why paying attention to what others are asking you about can be so helpful.

A really good way of identifying what you could be teaching other people is if it's something you are really curious about and find super-interesting. If you find something effortless that other people find quite complex, you're onto a winner. Your job in the online course you create is to take what you find simple and second nature and interpret it for other people. You break down the complexity so it's both easy for you to teach and easy for someone to pick up and run with.

If you get stuck on this, send an email to 20 close contacts or do a social media post simply asking people to let you know what they think you're best at. I know, you may feel a little uncomfortable doing that, but the answers will be insightful.

What do people ask me about? What am I known for?

_____

_____

_____

_____

Next, look at what people want. Keep in mind that what people say they want and what they actually want are sometimes very different, which can make it quite challenging to figure out. But for our big idea, we want to really drill down into what people want from us.

What do I find easy that others find challenging?

_____

_____

What is a problem my clients need to solve?

_____

_____

What can I provide that will reduce someone else's pain or difficulty?

_____

_____

What ignites my passion?

_____

_____

Don't skip what you're passionate about. There's no better feeling than doing something in life you're passionate about. You wake up feeling inspired by your own vision and dream. The self-fulfilment you experience when doing meaningful work is absolutely incredible. You show up joyfully every day. That joy will permeate all areas of your professional and personal life.

It's such a tragedy that so many people devote their lives and most of their waking hours to a career or occupation they're not passionate about, living dimmed-down versions of themselves. When you do something you're truly passionate about, you can help others to discover their own passion. Your sense of fulfilment, the way you light up each day, the energy you feel, is just fantastic. When I talk to people about building their own online courses—how they can take their idea, something they've long been dreaming about, and make it real, and make money doing it *and* still spend time with their family—they are super happy. Selfishly, that makes me feel wonderful too, because when you realise your dream is when I fulfil mine, and I'm very passionate about that. It allows me to live a better life while helping others to live better as well.

Go with that! Don't settle for something you trained for just because you don't want to 'throw away' your education, though it will all likely contribute to what you eventually do. If you feel uninspired by the course your career is taking, it's probably not the one for you. Leave it to someone else and aim for something that combines what people want and will pay for with what *you* love (see the Venn diagram in figure 1 for the sweet spot you should be aiming for).

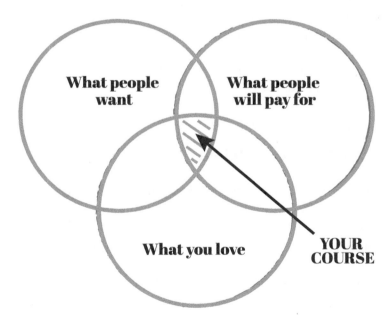

Figure 1: Finding your course's sweet spot

Let's look at some examples of people having paid for the idea already. First you need to ascertain whether or not there's a market for your big idea. It's much easier to sell something that people are already searching for. This doesn't mean you have to be a generalist; actually, quite the opposite.

One of the strangest online course success stories I've heard of is an entrepreneur who makes half a million dollars a year from running a tutorial on how to get your best eyebrows. She talks about how to trim them, grow them, colour them—all the different techniques for creating and maintaining your best brows. It amazed me to learn just how many women are into having perfect brows. Let me tell you, there are so many unlikely audiences in the world looking for the magic you could share. But your job will be much easier if there's already a pool of people who are looking for what you want to offer.

A good exercise is to use a tool called answerthepublic.com and type in a few variations of what you've brainstormed so far, to see how popular it is and what your future clients are already searching for.

By now your brain is firing and you're going, 'Yes! This is exactly what I want to do!' Let's do it.

Validating your idea

Some business strategists will disagree with this, but I believe too much analysis is overrated. Yes, you definitely need to analyse your plan and set yourself up for the best chance of success, but I can say with 100 per cent certainty that the online business you'll have in a few years will look very different from the one you started out with. This is because there are certain variables that you can't possibly know until it's actually out in the world.

You may have a product that generates great excitement in a pre-launch survey, only to find that when your offer is put out into the marketplace, no one wants to part with their cash to buy it. Conversely, you may have a product that people don't like to endorse or even talk about publicly, such as marriage counselling, but once launched your service finds a large and grateful market.

We'll look at some quick exercises to help you validate your idea but we won't go too far into it, because action beats research every single time. Your product won't be perfect to begin with, and the quicker you accept that the easier it will be, because it will take a little of the pressure off.

No matter what you do, and how much research you do, once it's out there you'll want to change it, adapt it, tweak it as you move forward. The market will validate it for you. What we want to do is to get the first offer out into the world as quickly and simply as possible so we can get that validation, then refine, improve and scale it.

When you first start out you may be brave enough to tell family and friends that you are creating an online course. Asking for people's opinions is a very useful exercise. Sometimes the feedback will be great, sometimes less so.

It's very easy to be swayed and discouraged by others' opinions. I want you to remember that most people aren't business owners and probably won't think it's a good idea simply because they themselves don't do it. Often loved ones will discourage you because they want to keep you safe. They don't want to see you fail, but their desire to protect you can be misdirected. Welcome feedback because sometimes it's highly valuable, but trust your own intuition. Go with what you believe in and what you want to deliver. That's always going to be the best thing to do.

Take some time out to complete the following validation exercise.

A validation exercise

1. Pick one of the best books written on your subject.

2. Look at the chapter outline.

3. Analyse the simplicity vs complexity of the content.

4. Read the reviews on Amazon and Goodreads.

Purpose of the exercise:

When putting a course together, it can be tempting to throw in as much content as possible. Don't mistake more content for more value. The value is in getting your clients' problems solved in the simplest way possible. Your aim is to deliver exactly what you need to get the desired result—no more, no less. Looking at a chapter outline is a really helpful way to see that, because it's already been proven. If it's a best-selling book, you know you're looking at an outline of something that already works. Look at that for inspiration and ideas of the different things you can use, the structure and how content-dense the information is.

After you've completed this exercise, go and do the same thing with the best websites on the subject:

- Who has the best online course? Who are the best thought leaders in the area?

- What is that person's *signature course*?

- Is it close to what you have?

- What is their *opt-in*? An opt-in is also known as a lead magnet. Put simply, it's a valuable resource offered to potential clients, such as a training video, checklist or workbook, that you give for free in exchange for the client's email address and permission to continue to market to them. Reviewing a variety of opt-ins on your competitors' websites will give you some ideas of what your audience is already looking for.

- Where is their traffic coming from? Google them to see all the media coverage they've had. Are they on TV or radio? Are they being invited as podcast guests? Are they bloggers?

Get to know your clients so well that you can spot the holes in other people's offers and do it better. Look for proof of what people are looking for, not just what they say they want.

During our 2018 gap year I travelled around the world with my family, frequently using a low-cost airline with a notoriously bad rap. (I know you know who I mean!) When they published the results of their customer feedback survey, it turned out that many passengers complained of lack of legroom and how uncomfortable and crammed together they were.

In response to what customers said they wanted, the airline introduced a cabin that added an extra 10 centimetres between each seat and extra legroom. They charged an extra hundred dollars for the tickets because they could now fit fewer seats on the plane. Every time we flew with this airline we found that cabin nearly empty. Most customers, although complaining vehemently about the lack of legroom, still wanted the cheapest possible option. They weren't willing to pay for the very thing they said they needed. Yes, people wanted more legroom, but the most important real problem the airline was solving for customers was to get them from A to B the cheapest way possible.

Look at your market and potential clients and read between the lines. Pay attention to what they're saying they want, but pay particular attention to the main problem they actually need solved and the value that is most important to them. You know your work intimately—you're the best at it—and you know your clients and what they most want.

Put yourself in their shoes and create the program that will deliver what they most want. As Henry Ford is purported to have said, 'If I had asked people what they wanted, they would have said faster horses'.

Creating your vision

To create the best course possible, you need to maintain your focus on the people you're serving. If you keep your clients at the front of your mind, always thinking about the challenges they face and the desires they have, and how you can bridge that gap and solve that problem, then you will always do a really good job. You will always demonstrate integrity and know you're doing absolutely the best you can.

It's a noisy world out there. Too many people are telling us things we don't need to know. One of the best things about social media is that everyone has a platform and a voice (it's also one of the most negative things, but we'll save that debate for another day). If you focus on speaking directly, clearly and concisely to your clients and their needs, your message will cut through the noise and really resonate.

We're doing these preliminary exercises before we actually get into the course creation so you're super clear on what it is you really want to create for the people you serve.

What is the goal of your course? What will members achieve?

_____

_____

_____

This is also known as your _transformation promise_. It says, 'I will get you from here at point A to there at point B'.

What positive impact can you have on your industry?

_____

_____

_____

I'm a purpose-driven person. I want my life to matter and I want to make a meaningful difference in the lives of others. At the end of my life I want people to know that I was here and that I made a positive impact. I want to make business easy and have a bucketload of fun while doing it. What impact do you want to have within your industry?

When participants complete your course, what positive impact will that have on their life?

_____

_____

_____

We can change many lives by focusing on having a positive impact on just one. It's so important to have conviction and believe in what you're doing. Think about the transformation promise of your course. If a client completed your course and achieved the goal you've set, how would that affect their life?

As I write this book I'm asking myself exactly that. It's what keeps me going when self-doubt threatens or I get distracted and want to run away from my computer. I know online courses have changed my life and the lives of so many others. Once you've finished your online course, you'll have won both location freedom and time freedom. You can work from anywhere and you can work around your children's schedules. If you want to work 10 hours one day and only an hour the next, you can. You'll have enough money, and you'll enjoy the sense of self-fulfilment. That's what it means for your life. For me, it's enough to drive me to do the work I do and continually risk failure by trying new things and stepping out of my comfort zone.

When members complete my course, what positive impact will that have on their community?

_____

_____

_____

I've talked about the many benefits for your life when you're running a million dollar micro business. The potential benefits for your community are even greater. It means you have the time and energy to give back to your community, so you may for instance be more involved in charitable work. When you're a happier human, that itself can snowball, impacting your partner, your children, even the person who works at the grocery store. This beautiful energy flows through to everyone in your orbit. Imagine what that will mean for your students' own immediate community if they're really successful in completing your course.

Values

We humans tend to be mission driven. Running your company, no matter how small or large, is so much easier when you and your team know why you're doing it. If you've worked in corporate, you may dismiss the company's mission statement as so many meaningless words that some external branding company came up with to stick on the lunch room wall and tick a box. But a clear mission statement is a valuable way to remind you what you're doing and why. It's simple and concise and will tell the world what you're here for.

The company I grew for a decade was called Begin Bright. With educational tutoring centres throughout Australia, our mission was displayed prominently in the waiting room of each centre. It was simple: 'To create happy, smart and confident children'. We knew exactly what we were there for. We knew who we were and who we weren't. Now my mission is 'To accelerate empowered, successful women who are building online empires'.

What is your company mission statement?

_____

_____

Your values drill down into what's important to you and your company. Being clear on your values will help you fulfil your mission.

Google 'values list examples' and you'll be flooded with beautiful character traits and qualities you can consider. I want you to narrow it down to your top 10 values (you can make a start using the space overleaf). Far from being hollow words, they provide you with a very useful guide. When you embrace really clear values, every decision you make becomes easier. When you're faced with something that you need to say yes or no to, if you look to your values, decision making becomes really easy, because if it fits into your values, it's a hell yes! If it doesn't fit into your values, then it's no. You know when to pass and when to go by whether or not something is congruent with your values. One of ours for my program Her Empire Builder is 'We will have a community of kind people only'. This is like saying we have a 'no arsehole policy' but put in a much nicer way! It does make it easier for me to select who comes into the group and who doesn't. It's a collaborative and supportive group, so if anyone doesn't want to play to that, it makes it really easy for me to say no. Once you define your values, you're really clear on who you want to be as an individual, what impact you want to make in your community, what impact you want to make on other individuals' lives, and what your company is going to represent.

<u>Company values:</u>

1. _____

2. _____

3. _____

4. _____

5. _____

6. _____

7. _____

8. _____

9. _____

10. _____

Personal business goals

We have been looking at the issue from the client's point of view — what we want them to be able to achieve as a result of doing our course. Now it's time to look at it from your own point of view, to examine what you personally want to achieve.

I've always been a massive fan of goal setting. I did my first Tony Robbins course when I was 16. I absolutely love it. Having clearly defined goals provides a roadmap for where I want to go and how I'm going to get there, a path to follow and a destination, rather than flying blind, flailing about and wasting time trying to think about what you want to do next.

In saying that, goal-setting techniques work differently depending on your psychology and what you best respond to. Some people set sky-high goals, which means the chances of actually achieving them are very small. But even setting overambitious goals means you can climb way higher than you would if you didn't have any clearly defined goals. The downside of that strategy is that you risk being perpetually disappointed, because you're setting goals you can rarely reach. If that sounds like you, and you feel demoralised by falling short rather than motivated, then *don't do it*. Set yourself achievable goals.

The most widely proven effective goal-setting strategy is to create bite-sized goals then set an action plan and just do it. Each time you set just the next step. Sure, you keep the whole big picture in the back of your mind, but we all know how life throws us curve balls. If we're too tied to a long-term plan, it can be difficult not to be dismayed when we're inevitably thrown off course. It's much easier and less stressful to focus on the next milestone you need to reach on the way to your main objective. Each milestone reached will boost your confidence, encouraging you to believe in yourself more and be bolder, and in this way your progress will start to accelerate. It's one reason why the first year of an online business is often quite slow—much slower than the success stories you so often read about. But in the second year your growth doubles, then it compounds, and within a few years you have a seven-figure business.

Of course you know yourself better than anyone does, so learn what strategy motivates you best to achieve what your heart most deeply desires, then have the discipline to stick with it. It's up to you to inspire yourself to continue this journey. Success is what happens when no one is watching. The work you do as an online entrepreneur is often not visible. It looks all show on the front end, but long-term success means continually going above and beyond for your clients behind the scenes. Only you truly know the effort you're putting in. You will be your own biggest cheerleader, so make sure you're set up and ready to cheer loudly!

The first goal we're going to set is your annual income goal. Too many people focus on impact rather than making money. Making an impact through your work is obviously something I'm really passionate about, as we've already talked about at length. But don't forget to focus on actually making money along the way. The primary purpose of a business is to be profitable.

The pursuit of wealth can be associated with greed or unprincipled behaviour. Let me tell you, wealth increases your ability to serve the community and the world. Identify what negative money beliefs you hold and work on letting them go. I've listed a few great books on this in the resources section at the end of the book. One way to serve more people is to make more money, because the more money you have, the greater impact you can have in the world. If you're going to do good things with it, then you should aim to make more money, and you can use your online business as a vehicle to do that.

What is your annual income goal? _____

Now I want to talk about work hours. 'Hustle' is a dirty word. I'm a reformed workaholic. Running my previous business, I worked double the hours I do now and I was constantly exhausted, and underpaid. You've probably heard the expression 'Work smarter, not harder'. I know when I used to hear it I'd feel as though my retinas might disconnect from my eye roll, but there is truth in it. Focus on what matters and forget the rest. I see people spending all day every day on 'busy work' rather than the work that actually makes a difference and propels the business forward. When you're working, ask yourself, would it actually make a difference if I didn't do this? And if your answer is no, *stop*. Focus your time on the highest returning activities and you will have the headspace to perform as your business needs you to, and to make good decisions, spot opportunities and take advantage of them.

When I ask people why they started their business the most common answer I get is they wanted more freedom. People may go into business ownership to reduce their work to 20 or 30 hours a week, but then there's always more to do and you can very easily fall back into the trap of overwork.

Set the goal for how many hours you're really, really happy working each week: _____

Okay, let's work out how you can actually hold the line when you reach that weekly limit. There will be weeks when you know you'll have to do more, such as in launch periods. Then there will be weeks when you need to work fewer hours. Aim consistently for what you're comfortable with. Anything after that can just wait until the next week or be delegated. In chapter 19, we look at your micro team to ensure you get the support you need to enable you to do this.

I like to tie a reward or celebration to the achievement of each goal I set. As the business owner, you are the only one who will pat you on the back. There's no one else to validate you or tell you that you did a good job. So you need a system in place that ensures you stop, recognise and reflect on your achievements and mark the milestone in some way. It provides you with important motivation, because in business we aim so high and there is always so much more we could be doing.

Breaking goals down into milestones and action steps, then tying a reward to each one, allows a pause in which you can acknowledge and celebrate the fact that you just made happen the very thing you set out to do.

You can fill in the table overleaf, or download your own copy.

GOAL:		Achieve by:
Action steps	**Achieve by**	**Reward**
1.		
2.		
3.		
4.		
5.		
6.		
7.		
8.		

Following are some good goals to set at this stage:

- Define your first online course.

- Set a date for your first course launch.

- Create your social media profiles.

- Build your website.

- Set up your business structure.

Think about your business in 12 months' time. If you were to commit to starting your million dollar micro business and follow the advice in this book, going full steam ahead, imagine what life could look like for you in 12 months. What does success look like for you? It's different for everyone so I want you to really think about what *your* goals are and what you are building towards. When designing your goals, really get into what *you* want. What would life look like if no one was watching? Think about things like what your day-to-day looks like. How many clients are you serving? How much time are you devoting to the business?

What my life will look like in 12 months' time:

_____

_____

_____

_____

_____

_____

I want you to think about your ideal world, because that's what we're going to create.

06

Set up your new business

Now it's time for the fun part—bringing this business baby to life! Let's make this thing real and start setting up your new business. Regulations will vary slightly in different jurisdictions, but here I'll cover the main areas that are applicable for all. By the end of this chapter, you will have what you need to officially establish your business.

Business name

A lot of people find coming up with the most apposite business name a challenge, but the hardest part is actually finding one that's available. In the era of domain parking, people register domain names in anticipation of future need or in order to resell them later. For some they've become a great investment, but this has made securing a fitting business name increasingly challenging.

Before you settle on your business name, check its availability for your:

- website address (URL)

- social media handles

- trademarks.

A good tool to use for this is namecheckr.com.

You may already have another business running. Say you've got a service-based business and you want to add an online course to that. You can do it under your existing business name, or you may opt to do it under a separate business name.

If your online program is something you want to continue running after you sell your existing business—or if you want to keep the two entities separate, which I definitely recommend—you need to create a new business.

Company name vs personal name

Some course creators will build their business on the back of a company name, others on yourname.com. Each option has merits, and your decision here will depend on your goal in the long term. If you're going to hire a large team and have other team members run sessions and play a part in the delivery of your products and services, then it makes sense to use a company name. However, if you are your business and people are purchasing access to your own expertise, then go with your personal name. You may feel uncomfortable with creating a 'me show', but humans buy from humans—you may as well embrace it! You can build a relationship and trust much quicker and easier when you personally represent your company rather than hiding behind a brand name with customers in the dark as to who runs it.

An objection I often hear is that a business under a personal name is hard to sell, but you're not building this type of business to sell. Sure, you'll develop a lot of IP and assets along the way, but your business is built on your expertise and your thought leadership. You are the secret sauce. No one else can replicate you. If you want to build a business to sell, this model isn't for you. Embrace the idea that you are the product here, and totally own it.

When you create a seven-figure online business you'll earn far more in the long run than you would if you built a traditional business from the ground up. When I was running my franchise company, for the first eight years I drew very little income, barely making minimum wage. I knew the sacrifice would be worth it because I was building something epic that could later be sold for multiple seven figures. Eventually, 13 years after inception, it did. In the online business world, I have made more money in my first three years than I did in my entire traditional business journey, including the sale price! Sure, I can't sell tinatower.com, but why would I want to?

Generally, then, you will trade under your own name and set up a company that is registered to operate the business. Your company will hold your personal name as a business name as well as the names of the courses you run. I recommend registering a domain name and protecting each of your course names as well, but we'll talk more about that later in the chapter.

Registering your business name

These are the steps to registering your business name:

1. Brainstorm all your ideas for naming your course and your company entity. Most likely you already have some ideas on this. Brain dump them all on paper or a giant whiteboard. Write down everything that comes to mind. Use a thesaurus for further inspiration.

2. Check the availability of the names. Be sure to check both locally and abroad, because as soon as you are operating an online business you are a global company, and the last thing you want is to discover you have inadvertently used names that are already registered in another country. Check domain registers and social media, do a trademark search then do a simple Google search to make sure.

3. Register the names according to the laws of your country and/or state.

Your business structure

This is simple: go to your accountant! Don't skimp at the set-up stage on establishing the company structure that's right for you and your specific situation. There are so many possible variations, so spending a few hundred dollars for professional advice is a great investment. It could save you way more than that down the line in taxes and restructuring costs.

Your accountant will also help you navigate your taxation registrations so you can start collecting money from clients as soon as your course goes live—yay!

Setting up your business banking and accounting software

I still remember the day I received my first business bank card. That official recognition was so exciting! As soon as you have your entity name sorted, go and open that account. If you like having all your accounts in one internet banking window, you may choose to stay with the bank you already use, or you may prefer to start from scratch.

When I started out in business I didn't mind going with different banks. I usually chose whichever bank offered the best deal at the time, knowing that all those expenses add up. Now I'm happy to pay a $10 fee to keep it all together, providing a more convenient internet banking portal and app.

As everything in your online business is automated and happens electronically, you'll never need to go into a bank. The transaction process will be:

1. Payment is received through your course platform (I use Kajabi for this).

2. The Merchant processes the transaction, most often through Stripe or PayPal.

3. The Merchant deposits the funds into your bank account.

4. The customer is automatically sent a receipt.

5. If you're in a country where you need to send a taxation invoice, then your Merchant will sync with a software product called Quaderno so the process happens automatically.

6. This will then sync with your accounting software (I recommend Xero).

I'm a big fan of doing what you're great at and outsourcing the rest, so I recommend using a bookkeeper to do all the technical app stacking and making sure everything is synced and reconciled correctly. The bookkeeper will also help you set up your accounting software.

Always keep your business and personal expenses separate. It's a good idea from a taxation point of view as well as a performance point of view that you start as you mean to continue. Perhaps you decide not to worry about setting everything up properly at the start, thinking you'll just start slow. Bugger that! Start with the right set-up to propel you towards your goals as quickly as you can.

Good bookkeeping allows you to see at a glance how the business is performing, and what is and isn't working, so you can make quick adjustments and achieve success more easily.

Action steps

Set up your business bank account.

Install and set up your accounting software.

Registering your domain name

GoDaddy is my domain provider of choice because they're easy to use, well known and trusted. Buy your root domain first. A root domain is the URL you mean to use as your main website. You can set up any other domains you purchase to redirect to that main root domain.

When you're domain shopping, I recommend investing in privacy protection, which will hide your contact details from online searches. It costs around $10 to $20 a year. It means you won't be on the Whois.com registry, which saves you from a lot of spam. When you go on a public database, you'll get loads of emails from people throughout the world offering their web services, SEO services and the like. I personally hate excess emails, so paying that small annual fee for domain privacy protection so I don't have to worry about being spammed is well worth it. If spam doesn't bother you, then maybe save the $20 there.

Don't worry about adding extras like hosting as your website will be on Kajabi and your email hosting through Google Workspace (formerly G Suite).

Protect your domain real estate! Every country has its own identifying extension; for example, in the US **.com**, in Australia **.com.au** and **.co.uk** in the UK. Because the US is the global leader in online programs, you should always register the .com no matter where you are. I like to get as many other different domain extensions as I can afford. To be able to protect your domain name in various countries throughout the world for a couple of years, around $20 is a worthwhile investment.

Action step

Buy your domain name(s).

Setting up Google Workspace for your emails

Now you have your business name and domain name, let's set up your email address.

I am a big fan of Google Workspace for email because it opens the door to so many other tools. You get access to Google Calendar and Gmail, so you can access your emails really easily. Google Docs allows you to collaborate with others on text documents. You can store all your course videos on Google Drive and keep your business systems manual on Google Sites. So for $5 a month per email address, Google Workspace is well worth it and definitely the way to go.

Go to workspace.google.com, hit Get Started and you'll be walked through the whole process. When entering your nominated main email address, you may want to use a generic customer service email address. For example, the main email address I use is **hello@tinatower .com**. It's the one I started out with so I could enter that address on all our subscriptions and use it for customer service email, because I knew that as soon as I was able to afford an assistant, they would be monitoring that address. I then set up my personal email address as an alias. You can create as many aliases as you like. You might use hello@, yourname@, podcast@ or marketing@. All of these derivatives will make you feel like you have lots of staff but they're all coming through to the one email address. As your company grows, you can split them off into their own email accounts. Setting up aliases now will save you money on additional accounts later.

Again, this is something you could do cheaper without having an email address linked to your domain name, but let's be super professional and set it up properly from the beginning.

Action step

Register on Google Workspace and set up your custom email address.

Setting up Dropbox

You can share documents by using Google Docs through Workspace, but I also like to have a Dropbox folder set up. It provides an easy way to share, store and upload your files, which you'll be doing a lot of, and for a certain amount of data it's free. I keep copies in both Google Drive and Dropbox as a backup in the unlikely (but possible) event that one software system fails. OMG, imagine losing all the resources and video recordings you've created over the years because of a system malfunction. Eeek!

Dropbox links are a super easy way to keep things nice and organised. Also, when you're uploading files to your online course website, they load a gazillion times faster from Dropbox than from a folder on your computer. It's absolutely essential to be organised right from the very beginning. In the course creator's Dropbox you will set up, as a bare minimum, the following folders:

- Branding assets

- Social media posts

- Promotional images

- Course video content with modules and lessons in organised subfolders

- Corresponding worksheets and resources for course videos

- Product images.

You can tell I love organisation, right? But being able to find the things you're looking for quickly and easily saves *so* much time. Your future self will thank you, I promise.

Dropbox also has Selective Sync, which means once your whole course has been loaded onto your platform, you can take it off your computer's hard drive and store it 'online only' in the cloud. This means your computer can keep powering on at top speed without giant files slowing it down.

Action step

Register for Dropbox and set it up on your computer.

Protecting your IP

You've already taken great steps to protect your IP through registration, but I want to take it one step further.

A lot of people worry about the theft of their stuff once they have uploaded it. And it will happen, time and time again. My attitude is just don't worry about it. They do it because you're really good at what you do. So you can look at it from that point of view. It's also theft and illegal, but people will still do it. There's only so much protection you can count on, so if your plan is to go really big with your course (and I know it is), I recommend talking to a trademark lawyer.

Get on Google and research the relevant regulations, both locally and overseas. It blows my mind that there's no global trademark system, but a preliminary chat with a trademark lawyer will help you decide whether this is a step you want to take. Registering a trademark is a lengthy and expensive process, so you will need to be absolutely sure of the name and future direction of your business.

You can protect a lot with a trademark, but it won't stop people downloading and copying your stuff, so there's no point in wasting any energy on that. Some people dismiss it as no more than a sign of flattery. Try to take it as a compliment. It's worth remembering that people copy you because they don't have original ideas of their own. So as you continue to evolve and learn and do better, they'll continue to chase after you. They can copy what you do, but they can't copy who you are. Also, there's a lot of very similar content out there. It's how it is delivered that's so different, so embrace who you are and focus on sharing your gifts with the world.

Action step

Consult a trademark lawyer about the protections available to you.

Budget

People tell me that spreadsheets scare them. Learn to love them! I did very basic maths in high school and didn't do all that well. I knew that to be successful in business I had to learn to know my numbers and work with them, so I practised and practised. Now, I'm a ninja with a Google Sheet and I love my beautiful budget.

Of all of the different businesses I have run, my online business is the simplest in terms of marketing and structure, and definitely requires the lowest budget. When you're starting a traditional business, there are so many expenses to take into account and so many unexpected costs. This is less an issue for an online business. It's pretty easy to control the budget at the beginning, as there's not much that can really blow out in terms of costs (unless you develop an unhealthy Facebook advertising habit!).

Download the digital budget planner sheet at milliondollarmicro business.com and start inputting numbers particular to your business.

Following are some typical set-up expenses you'll encounter. (Turn to chapter 17 on automation for an explanation of the ongoing monthly subscriptions you may have.)

Set-up expenses:

- Education and training $2000

- Business registration $500

- Domain registration $125

- Trademark lawyer consultation $250

- Canva templates $100

- Logo design $500

- Filming equipment $1000

- Launch marketing $1000

Total set-up cost = $5475

Ongoing monthly subscriptions*:

- Bookkeeper $200

- Kajabi $149

- Google Workspace $10

- Monday.com $63

- Canva $14

- Xero accounting software $25

Figures are current at time of writing and are estimates only.

- StreamYard $25

- Virtual office phone number $20

- Calendly $8

- Adobe Audition $43.99

- Libsyn $20

- Zoom $25

- Otter $10

- Later $12.50

- Dropbox $20

- Quaderno $50.

Take, for example, filming equipment. You could create your first videos and do your launch using the phone in your pocket. Or you could go all out and hire a professional recording studio for $4000 a day. And there are many options in between, which is why it's important to create your own spreadsheet with your actual costs, which will depend on your budget.

I advise people launching their first online programs to strive to achieve in revenue in their first launch whatever they spent on their set-up expenses.

Your first launch income goal is: $_____

For business success, a good rule of thumb is to spend only what's vitally necessary while making as much money as you can. As with time management, spend on the things that matter, and forget the rest. If it boosts your brand and/or your sales, then it's a worthwhile investment. If not, always question whether it's vital or just something you want. Remember, revenue is for vanity and profit is for sanity. It doesn't matter how much revenue you have if you spend it all on expenses. Focus on creating and widening that gap so you develop wealth to invest in line with your values and future goals.

Action step

Create your budget spreadsheet so you know what to allow for your start-up and what to aim for as your income goal.

07

Map out your signature course

Okay, let's build this. It's time to map out your signature course. By the end of this chapter you'll know what your course is called, what the modules are and what points you're going to cover in each of them. It's going to be real—it's happening for you now, so get ready! Let go of any self-limiting beliefs, let go of your fear, and start creating your awesome, life-changing, world-changing signature course.

Your course creation road map

Your signature course is the first thing you'll launch out into the world. You may already have about 20 potential courses in mind! Resist trying to do everything at once. Launch one thing well before allowing yourself to turn your attention to the next one. I like to set a benchmark. For example, if your goal is to reach $10 000 from your first course, then focus on that and only that until you reach that goal. Only then should you allow yourself to launch your second course. Some very successful course creators, people like Denise Duffield-Thomas (you'll meet Denise later in the book) and Amy Porterfield, have experienced massive success by refining and relaunching the same signature course again and again, year after year. The simplest way to start in the online course world is with a six- to eight-week course on doing what you do best. Remember the exercise in chapter 5 where we found the sweet spot where what you love, what you're good and what people will pay for intersect? That's what you'll launch as your signature course and what you'll be known for.

What will you call your signature course?

_____

You've already established the transformation promise for your course. That's what your course promises your clients—what will take them from where they are now to where they want to be in the simplest and quickest way possible.

You need to break down your course into modules. These are the main steps students will take to achieve the outcome. Each of those modules should be broken down further into lessons. Each lesson will cover the points you need to convey and include accompanying action steps. Action steps are vital to student success. I've seen too many people complete online courses only to leave at the end wondering what they should actually be doing. Make it as simple as possible for your clients to implement each of the lessons by providing actionable and achievable steps throughout. Add further resources for each lesson, such as a quick reference checklist, an ebook or an audio file.

The most important outcome of your course is for students to get the result for which they purchased your program. You will create better content by always keeping that top of mind.

How best to sort out your content will depend on how your mind works best. Some people love a spreadsheet (you'll find a spreadsheet for this exercise at milliondollarmicrobusiness.com). If you're a visual person, you might prefer to brain dump all your module and lesson ideas onto Post-it notes then arrange and rearrange them on the wall.

Effective education is all about bridging the gap between where your students are now and where they want to be. Because this is what you're best at, it's most likely something you find relatively simple. The challenge is in clearly communicating your expertise to people who are new to it. Once you've mapped out your lessons, take another look at them and ask yourself if they can be further simplified or presented differently to increase their clarity and student success.

Course delivery

How you deliver your content will vary depending on your industry, customer expectations and preferences, and your personal style. There are a few different ways you can set up content delivery:

1. All content is made available at the time of purchase.

2. Content is made available on a certain date.

3. Content is drip-fed at intervals.

4. Content is available for a fixed time only.

Let's look at each of these options.

All content is made available at the time of purchase

This is the option I choose for my short courses because I serve business owners, who are time poor and want what they need, like, yesterday. If I was to withhold content from my clients, they would not be happy. They like to purchase the course they need and then go through it at their own pace when their schedules allow.

I've had people buy my eight-week course and smash it out that weekend, all in one hit. Others have taken a year to get through the content. This flexibility allows clients to set their own pace.

Content is made available on a certain date

If you're live launching a program and providing support throughout, as in a weekly live webinar, and you want to build a sense of camaraderie among your students, then a restricted start date and staged roll-out is fabulous.

Take Stacey, who runs a weight loss and nutrition course. She knows that customer success is enhanced when students have accountability and a support system. When she launches her program she restricts access so people who sign up see only a welcome video; then, once the course is closed for enrolments, everyone gains access to the content at the same time and they can work through it together.

Content is drip-fed at intervals

Learning something new can be overwhelming. Drip-feeding content is a great way to avoid overloading students with all your content. The risk I run when I allow access to all of my content at once is that someone will respond, 'Oh my goodness, that's a lot! How am I ever going to get through it all?'

Kylie runs a course to help small business owners do their own bookkeeping. It's a lot of complex information and can easily psych people out if they feel like they're falling behind. So Kylie drip-feeds her content. When a new student signs up they gain access to module 1 and can work through that for a week. Seven days later, module 2 appears automatically in their library, with succeeding modules released week by week for the duration of the program. Drip-feeding content is a sensational way to help stage people through to completion. It also means students can't skip through content. You can lock your content so one module must be completed before the following one is accessible.

You can choose whether to do a daily, weekly or monthly drip, or whatever other interval you think most suitable.

Content is available for a fixed time only

'Lifetime access!' is a value-add you'll see on sales pages for online courses. I'm not a fan. Our number one goal with our online course is to deliver on the transformation promise to the student. Open-ended access may seem like you're offering good value, but it often provides a disservice. Course completion rates sit around 3 to 5 per cent. That is abysmally low. You can't expect testimonials and word-of-mouth referrals from people who don't actually complete your course. All the design and staging of your course is built around helping to make it as easy as possible for students to complete it and get the positive result they signed up for.

My first short course was eight weeks long, but I gave people 12 months' access because I knew that sometimes life just happens, preventing them from completing it in the time allowed. An automated email was programmed to go out three weeks before students' access expired at the one-year mark. What I found was a flurry of people jumping in and completing the course shortly before the cut-off date. So I made the decision to reduce access from 12 months to 12 weeks. That may seem counterintuitive but actually it provides more value, because the goal of your course is to achieve the result. Twelve weeks' access still builds in an extra four weeks to allow for the unexpected, but students can keep up their momentum because they know it's a three-month program. My course completion rate rose from 57 per cent to 78 per cent with this one small change.

When deciding how to make your course available, think about what you want students to have achieved by the end of the course. Make sure you stage your content so they gain the best result possible.

Creating community

Humans are social beings who crave connection with like-minded souls. Through coaching online course creators, I have encountered many unexpected and unlikely online communities that are passionate about their subject and delighted to find one another—from organic bee farmers to self-love gurus, yogis to tech entrepreneurs, flute teachers to felt makers.

I'm a big fan of creating a tribe around your course and your community. This is vital for you if you're running a membership or if you have other programs they can advance to. People come for your course but stay for your community. You've brought together a group of people with shared interests and values. They're on the same journey and are focused on the same result. Fostering that community will benefit both your business and your members. Studies have shown that when you're trying to do something new or hard, having an accountability buddy can increase your chances of success from 5 per cent to 60 per cent. Your students provide one another with support and accountability.

The most common place to maintain your community is in a closed, 'members only' Facebook group. It's really easy to use, and at the time of writing there are more than 2.7 billion Facebook users, so the chances are high that your client is familiar with the platform. If you're building your online course using Kajabi, they have an inbuilt community feature that allows you to conduct conversations away from the distraction of social media. The downside is that most people are already on Facebook so it's much easier to get high engagement there. If you have a client base that isn't especially comfortable chatting on social media, like a lot of professional services, then using the inbuilt community feature is a good option. But by creating a community off social media, you're adding an extra challenge around luring people across to that community.

Either way, your challenge is how to engage your community and keep them active and interested. In a world of information overload you need to offer useful engagement and content without stepping into information overload. I love a good system, but you don't want to overly systemise human engagement. Posting every Monday, 'What are you working on this week?' and every Friday, 'How did you go this week?' is boring snoring and your audience will disengage from you really quickly. Remember that social media platforms are all about being social. You're a human working with other humans and you must be relevant to what they're going through in your course right now.

Maybe you already participate in some amazing Facebook groups. Pay attention to what they do to keep the culture great, and draw inspiration from their example. Keep in mind how you can regularly and consistently deliver value to your members.

I'm part of a worldschooling travel group. One popular weekly post (when the world isn't in a pandemic) is, 'Where are you today?' And every week people put up photos of themselves and their children in locations around the world. That thread is absolutely ginormous, and obviously hugely interesting and relevant for the participants of that group. Think about what's going to be really relevant to your community and what people are going to engage with.

Create a list and brainstorm as many discussion ideas as you can, so when you do launch your course, you already have a bank of material relating to what you're going to talk about each week as your course progresses. Creating this as you're building your course is much easier and it will take the pressure off when you're connecting with your students and scrambling for what to say.

If you're dripping content and everyone is working through your program at the same time, introduce challenges and prizes. Amy is running a course on how to run Facebook ads. As her students progress, she sets a challenge to help them implement what they've learned in that module. They then share their results in the Facebook group, along with any roadblocks they've come up against, so they can work through them together. The results are far better than if they were left to it, with no one checking in to see how they're going or prompting them for progress.

Prizes and incentives to mark the achievement of different milestones are a great motivator. Everyone loves a present and good old-fashioned acknowledgement. It's an awesome bonus, if your program and profit allow for it. Kajabi is a company that does this really, really well. When you make your first thousand dollars, they send you a shirt that carries the message 'kajabi hero'.

When I got my t-shirt I just thought it was a nice gesture. Then I learned there are hero milestones and different prizes as your courses get more successful—and the competitive girl in me soon came to love it! You get a shirt, a hat, socks, a jacket—all sorts of things, so there are surprising numbers of people walking around in Kajabi gear. It's a win–win! You feel great being acknowledged for your super progress, and it's incredible advertising for the company as it encourages people to share it on social media and wear it with pride.

Look at some of the communities you're in and how they engage people. Then think about how you can best engage your community so you can create a really fabulous tribe who will support one another along their journey through your programs.

Action steps

Name your course.

Decide on your content availability.

08
Develop your course content

I hope you're feeling the gathering momentum now and your brain is firing with all the future possibilities for your online empire. Now it's really starting to take shape, it's time to stop thinking about it and preparing for it and start actually developing and recording your first signature course. This is where that fear can really come into play! If you've never filmed yourself before, you're going to feel all kinds of silly when you first start doing it. Don't worry, we all do! As with everything, it takes practice to become comfortable with it, and you only get comfortable after you get started.

In this chapter I'll cover the equipment you need (and it's a lot less than you think). We'll look at how to figure out camera angles for filming video and when to use different approaches such as *face to camera* and *filming your screen*.

Future options

As I've mentioned, one of the hardest things early on is to start with only one online course. You'll have ideas for multiple courses, and that's okay; just keep the rest in mind for the future. When developing this first course, think about what you want people to do once they have completed the course. That way you'll seed your content with ideas you can develop down the track for graduates of this first course. A common strategy is to offer membership after your course so graduates can stick around and continue to learn from you and be part of the community.

Perhaps you want to offer a more advanced program for graduates, or maybe this course is the big kahuna, huge and meaty. After you've reached your critical goal with this first course, you could make a series of smaller, more affordable and attainable courses.

Memberships

As you develop your course, keep in mind where your clients will progress to next. I love memberships. I love being a part of them and I love running them. You get to know people and to learn from those who speak your language and have the experience you need to access to propel you to where you want to go in that area of expertise. If your industry allows for a membership model, then go for it! It gives you that magical Monthly Recurring Revenue (MRR), a key metric you'll often hear discussed in online course communities. It is much easier to love up and keep happy your current clients than it is to attract new ones. I always prefer serving fewer people to a higher level and forming deep relationships than having a churn of new clients. Each month you'll continue to collect your membership fees and have an ongoing cash flow you can depend on. As you launch your short courses, they provide you with that bulk bonus income.

I see memberships for many different types of businesses, from weekly yoga videos to meal plans to positive affirmation for children—all sorts of different things. My membership vehicle is Her Empire Builder and is for women already making six figures in their online business who want to accelerate past seven figures. It features business knowledge and strategy, mindset, guest experts, resources and events. I started my Mastermind Membership in 2020 because I had so many graduates of my short courses asking, 'Okay, so we're done, now what?' They were looking to do what I do and wanted to continue learning and to stay connected, so I created the space for that. Once you start, your customers will tell you exactly what they want.

There are many different membership structures you can explore. I could fill a book on that alone! If it's helpful to your clients and if you're adding massive value, it's a great idea, because it provides you with ongoing revenue and an opportunity to keep adding resources and content as you're learning and growing.

Coaching and consulting

One-to-one coaching and consulting can be a valuable add-on when you first launch your course. I now charge a substantial coaching fee, but when you're starting out the most important thing is to build a solid reputation in your industry, so you'll do a little more for a little less, until you reach that critical goal and you can start to adjust your strategy accordingly.

One of the main reasons we go into online courses is to create more leverage in order to move past that 'time for money' trade. That's most likely the reason you picked up this book. If you've already been running one-to-one coaching, the transition into one-to-many courses is beautiful, because you already have a reputation and don't have to start building your personal brand from zero. Although courses allow you more leverage and scalability, it's good to keep some individual contact. Personally, I love doing one-to-one coaching. I always set aside a few spaces for this so I can keep connected with people, because I like to know people well and help them on a personal level, to have that deep connection and see them thrive. If that's something your business can benefit from, and you have sufficient expertise and credibility, it's something that could really help both your business and your clients.

When I ran my first few webinars to sell my course, I added a bonus offering: if people joined within an hour of the webinar, they would receive a free, hour-long, one-to-one consultation with me. When I ran that first webinar and while I was still talking the notification popped up that I'd just made my first sale, it was an exciting moment! Providing that extra element at the beginning allowed me to form a deeper relationship with my students so I could really understand their pain points and the things they were getting most stuck on, and create future content that anticipated those issues.

Content creation

There are a lot of different modalities you can use to film your online course. The main ones are both simple and easy, which is why we're going to use them! They are:

- face to camera

- presentation mode

- screen share.

Face to camera

Here you set up your camera and talk directly down the barrel. It's great for shorter videos and especially good for the welcome video to each new module. Putting your face out there from the start allows people to connect with you more easily and quickly. It may feel as though it's all about you, but it's not. It's about the person who is on their phone or computer somewhere watching you and trying to learn what you're teaching. The truth is, they have a greater chance of success when they can see you, so you must put yourself out there. Don't be the person who just talks over the top of slides. So boring! Remember, this is about student success, so do what you have to do to make that happen. Here's a checklist for when setting up for face-to-camera sessions:

- camera

- microphone

- a chair if you want to be seated

- a suitable backdrop, such as a bookcase (keep it simple, uncluttered and on brand)

- good natural lighting (facing a window is best) or artificial lights.

Presentation mode

If you're an interactive person, you can set up a whiteboard and a wider screen angle, and present to the camera while illustrating your points on the whiteboard. This is just like filming how you would teach a normal, in-person workshop for your clients.

Screen share

If you're demonstrating how to do something on your computer or you want to use slides, share your screen. Remember to keep the camera on as well so students can always see your face. It's harder to hold the viewer's attention when talking over slides with no video, so show yourself. The easiest programs to use are Zoom and Loom. Zoom shot into prominence around the world during the COVID-19 pandemic. You can run a session sharing your screen and video and record it with no participants, then upload the video recording to your course.

Nayda, who runs yoga lessons, uses a combination of modalities. In some she's seated and talking to the camera about yoga; in others she films herself doing the yoga poses so the other teachers can learn them.

Most of the content delivery I do is through face to camera. I use a lot of screen grabs. I very rarely talk over the top of slides, because like most people I find it really boring. It's always good to keep the component of you talking as large as possible.

Think about what combination will be best for your course, content and client. Look at the lessons you've already mapped out and write next to each one what modality you're going to use to film it, so you can expand on your plan.

Resources to accompany your content

While creating your content keep your focus on student success. As you're going through, ask yourself what resource you could create that would make this easier for your student. I recently took a course in organic vegetable gardening. It was a long course that covered many different technical aspects, but one resource provided was a one-page PDF that you could print out and stick on the wall. It was a planting calendar. Each month it showed what seasonal vegetables you could be planting. It's a simple but amazing resource that ensures that I implement what I've learned over the long term.

Resources to accompany your course could include:

- guides

- checklists

- interactive spreadsheet

- swipe copy

- reports

- templates

- cheat sheets

- planner or calendar.

Action step

Decide on the modality you will use to film each of the lessons in your course and what resources you will include in each module.

At the end of each lesson, include an action step that moves students forward to the next level.

Recording your course

If you've been implementing as you go, your whole course is now mapped out. Wowsers, that's got to feel good!

Getting into the right psychological state is one of the most important prerequisites when recording your course, especially if all this is new to you. Once you are set up and ready to go and about to hit record, you may just want to run a million miles in the other direction. It helps to remind yourself why you're doing this. It's about the people you're engaging with, not about you.

When I started to record my first online course, I was petrified about being judged. People would see all of the parts of me that I didn't like. I should probably just stop and lose five kilos before recording! Oh come on, we've all been there, right? In reality, no one notices those things we see and criticise in ourselves, or if they do they don't care. They're there for your knowledge and your inspiration. They're thinking about how relevant it is to them and their own lives. I have a ritual I go through to get myself in the right frame of mind. I do this before I record a video, run a masterclass, step onto a stage, hit record on a podcast or anything else that requires me to forget about the world outside, and to show up and serve. The positive energy you demonstrate will impact how your content is received, so it's important to communicate that energy.

Music is one of the simplest and quickest ways to change your mental state. When creating your first course, choose a course theme song that will fire you up, helping you to feel strong and capable, and play it before each of your recordings. Other techniques you could use to change your state that take a little longer are meditation, a brisk walk or a swim. Think about the things in your life that make you feel good and use them to help you show up as your best self on your recordings.

Time and again, people I've coached do all the planning conscientiously then, when it's time to record the course and make it real, they fall back on every excuse under the sun to delay the next, most important step. If you're feeling apprehensive about filming yourself, one way around it is to tell yourself it's only a practice run. You're never going to publish this one, so you can hit record and just practise it. By taking the pressure off yourself, you may just find that at least one of those practice runs is pretty darn good.

Some people find it easier to step in front of the camera than others. Seeing me now, many would assume I find it super easy, but I still get nervous before hitting record, because it's always so important to me to do a good job and I know how many times it's going to be watched, whereas at the start no one is watching you as you learn! I find it easier to think of it as a performance. I get my game face on, like Beyoncé does with Sasha Fierce, and I perform. That doesn't mean I'm not being myself; it means I'm illuminating the parts of me I want to. I let go of all of the insecurities I carry around in my normal life and I step into my power. I stand tall, I believe in myself and I go for it.

The biggest mistake you can make is to read from a script. In our equipment list in the next few pages I have listed a teleprompter, but even then I would never use a full script. It takes special skill to read text and have it sound natural and spontaneous. You know yourself that listening and watching someone who is in flow and rolling along naturally is a completely different experience from listening to someone read a speech, such as a presentation, word for word. List your key points in each lesson, and perhaps some power quotes, then trust yourself and your knowledge. It makes for a far better experience for your audience. If you don't have a teleprompter, use a computer screen or even a piece of paper as your prompter.

If you're dissatisfied with the production quality of your videos, you can always refilm them when you start making money from your courses. Start as simply as you can and get great results and you'll be bringing in that professional film crew in no time.

The other day I saw a little video from a branding coach. If you're going to be a branding coach, then obviously you've got to be right into the polish. She was talking about how to be confident on camera. A lot of it focused on her selling fake eyelashes and breaking out the blow dryer and the whole kit and caboodle, which I really don't agree with. I think you should be authentically you. If you do a daily blow dry and wear fake eyelashes whenever you go out, then awesome, do that in the video. But don't aim to look like someone you're not, because it means you're not being congruent. If you're not being congruent, you'll feel uncomfortable and you won't present as well as you would if you were being yourself.

Also, all this fuss about appearance makes the filming a really big deal and needs a lot more effort. Spending an hour or two getting a blow dry and buffing yourself up before you sit down to record can really slow you down. You'll find reasons why you can't go ahead today because, you know, after all that preparation you've only got two hours to film, then you've got to pick the kids up from school or whatever else life is throwing at you. Make your recording process as easy and straightforward as possible.

The way to make filming easy and achievable is just to be yourself. Show up as you are, so whenever you feel inspired and in the zone you can grab your equipment, sit down and rock and roll. Be presentable, of course, but be *you*.

I have quite volatile skin. I have days where I have pimples and I will not record because no one wants that to be immortalised on film. We all have days that, for whatever reason, we know are not going to work, and that's okay. In everyday life I don't pack on a lot of makeup. I've just never been that big on it. When filming I use mascara and lip gloss because that's what I wear every day and I want to look and feel like me. I don't want to have professional makeup caked on my face, then one day I show up to an event looking like I always do, and someone wonders what happened to my face! Be comfortable in your own skin, be who you are and embrace that.

Now you've got that sorted, your next challenge is finding the time to do the filming in a quiet environment when you're feeling 'on'. As you become a course creator, batching is going to be your best friend. Batching allows you to get more done in less time. When I first started online courses, I thought I'd just do an hour every morning. But I found that dipping in and out wasn't the easiest way to do it. I need to go into the zone of it. Once I'm in that zone I like to get it all done so I can move onto the next thing.

If you want to maximise your time, embrace batching. Plan everything out beforehand, including all your notes, your slides, the handouts, the descriptions, then sit down and just go for it.

The downside of batching is that by the end of the day you can be heartily sick of your own voice and drained of the energy expended by your inner Sasha Fierce. As harsh as it sounds, one of the keys to being able to do good video is to get over yourself. Let go of your ego and focus on your clients. Look at it from a teaching rather than a personal point of view.

Avoiding the trap of perfectionism

We are all perfectly imperfect. Your video recordings won't be 100 per cent flawless because none of us are flawless. If you're continually striving for the unattainable you'll never get to launch this baby out into the world. Go for progress over perfection.

Say you're recording and you get a little tickle in your throat and you pause for a couple of seconds and take a sip of water, do you edit it out? Do you stop the video and go back and start it all again? No. Just be natural and keep going. Our everyday conversations aren't perfectly polished. We stumble, forget what we mean to say, get sidetracked and distracted. That's what humans do. And that authenticity makes video that's much more enjoyable to watch. When you're comfortable, people feel that energy and are more comfortable watching you.

The act of purchasing your course is quite a personal one. People will only do so if they agree with you and believe your values align with theirs and you communicate in a way that makes sense to them. I'm a business strategist and author. Women who set great store by a super-polished image, wearing sky-high heels and little dresses, bouffant hair and a tonne of makeup, are probably not going to be into me, because I'm more about walking barefoot on a beach in Fiji, playing with my kids, going for a swim if I get hot—and communicating in a really easy, honest way. Customers will gravitate towards what you naturally project. By being yourself consistently, you will attract the right tribe for you. One isn't better than another, but you need to find *your* tribe. When I'm learning from different people, two presenters could be offering near-identical content but if I resonate more with one than the other, that's who I'll choose to go with.

Soon after my podcast first launched, I received an email from a man who wanted to bring to my attention how often I giggled. He wrote:

Hi Tina,

Your new podcast sounds great and helpful, but I've noticed that you giggle frequently during it. I don't know if you're nervous or always amused by something. I have no problem with people being happy, but as a listener, this giggling makes it hard to take you seriously. Hope this feedback is valuable.

Oh my. When I read that I had no words. But here's the thing: he's not my listener. I actually don't *want* him to listen. What is an annoying giggle to one person makes another smile. One person may find my voice irritating, where someone else may find it soothing and encouraging. You're never going to please everyone so make sure you're presenting in a way that pleases you.

Now get out the camera and have a little practice—I'm pretty sure you have one in your pocket or your handbag right now. A good place to start is with your welcome video, because it's so fun. As soon as someone signs up for your course they will be directed to this video. Welcome them in and tell them what to expect from your course. It should be under one minute long and should simply reassure your new client that they made the right decision and are in the right place. Go on, hit record and see what you've got!

Course video lengths

Remember that more is not necessarily more valuable. A 60-minute lesson isn't inherently worth more than one that lasts 10 minutes. Studies from the past year suggest that our attention span is falling, so 5 to 15 minutes is a great length for your videos. Structure them so each lesson video contains a new idea. This makes them much easier to digest. Most students now consume course content on their phone whenever they have a small window of opportunity. If your video lasts an hour, they are more likely to put it away for later. Obviously this will depend on the subject area, so always look at it from your clients' point of view and what is likely to be best for them.

By organising it in bite-sized chunks, you'll give your students the best chance of completing the course successfully. Online learning means taking out any fluff. In-person workshops or programs tend to have a lot of fluff and fillers. There are ice-breakers and housekeeping and lots of breaks. In online learning you get to the point as quickly as possible. Your students are coming to you for tangible, actionable information that they can implement to achieve their desired goal, so don't waste 10 minutes talking about anything that's not going to help them get there.

Equipment

Brace yourself for the equipment list, because it's extensive. Your essentials are a camera or phone and a laptop or computer … That's it!

You can get carried away and invest in a lot more, and if you have the start-up funds I recommend you do so. But a small budget will not stop you from creating your million dollar micro business. Start small, make some money as soon as you can, then invest in higher quality equipment that makes your life a little easier.

Here I'll list the equipment I use and recommend so you have somewhere to start, but test everything out, do your research and find out what works best for you. You can find the links to each of these products at milliondollarmicrobusiness.com. As I've said, most items on this list aren't essential to start with, but they're things I have in my course creator's kit.

Camera phone

The cameras on today's phones are exceptionally good. If you're starting out and you have a phone released any time after 2020, the camera will be sufficient for recording your course videos.

Canon EOS M3 digital SLR camera

I love this little handbag-size DSLR because it's great for images for marketing purposes and for filming with super-sharp resolution. I bought my Canon specifically for doing videos because they are crisp and the sound quality is really good. If I'm filming face to camera and sitting less than 1.5 metres away from the camera indoors, then the filming can be done without a microphone. It also holds a lot of video. The way I like to record, as I've mentioned, is by batching. I have an adapter that allows me to put the battery in and plug it into a power socket so I don't have to keep recharging the battery, otherwise it will go flat in about one and a half hours. When you're buying a new camera, get one that you can also connect to the mains so it will have power for as long as you do.

Tripod

For a while when I started I would just sit the camera on top of a pile of books or on a shelf. Now I take my tripod around with me everywhere. It makes content creation much quicker and easier to set up.

MacBook Pro laptop

Every course creator needs a good laptop. I'm an Apple girl all the way; I use a MacBook Pro because I have so many files on there. You will be creating a heap of video, graphic design, photos and other resources, and you need a computer that can handle all that data. I'll also be encouraging you to start a podcast, so you need something that has both the processing power and the storage space to handle all of it with ease. Macs all come with iMovie, which is the program I use for editing my videos and is super simple to use.

Many of my friends who run online courses send their videos off to be edited. I do it myself. Again, it's very simple to upload from the camera straight into iMovie. I simply cut off the start and the end. Here's an insider tip that will save you a lot of time and confusion: When I record a video, I hit go and I say what module it is. Say I'm on module 4, lesson 4. I hit record and say '4.4'. Then when I upload all of the videos to the computer, I know which is which. Say the module when you're recording, then you can just cut that bit off the start when you're editing and save it with that file name.

Rode lapel mic

If you need a microphone, a Rode lapel mic will suffice for both course videos and your first podcast. The downside is that you'll have a cord. If you want no cord, you'll have to invest in a Rode Filmmaker kit.

Rode Filmmaker

This is what you'll need if you're creating videos in which you're moving around a lot—say, you're a yoga instructor or presenting from a whiteboard. One attachment goes on the camera and the other in your pocket.

Rode shotgun mic

If you're sitting straight in front of the camera but a couple of metres back, a shotgun mic will attach to the top of your DSLR and pick up your sound wonderfully well.

Boom mic arm

If you don't want to use a Filmmaker and you have a shotgun mic, you can set up a boom mic to hang overhead just off-camera. This will give you clear crisp sound without your needing to clip on a microphone.

Elgato Key Light

Natural light is the best kind of light for filming. If you can face a window and have natural, filtered light coming through, that looks gorgeous. In the absence of that, you have a plethora of lighting options. I love the Elgato Key Light because of its many options for light temperature and brightness levels.

Neewer video lighting kit with softbox diffusers

These are much bigger than the key light so if you want a light box set up on both sides, this is a great option. They're powerful lights with diffusers and you have a lot of flexibility with tone too.

Rode Podcaster mic

Rode has a large range of podcast mics so get the one that suits you best—they're all really good. I use mine when I'm recording straight onto the computer over Zoom or Loom. You'll also use it down the track for running webinars and podcasting.

Logitech Brio 4K webcam

Using a Mac with a pretty decent inbuilt camera, I never thought I'd need a webcam—until I got one! Oh my gosh, it makes everything look so much nicer. My skin looks fresh and dewy, and the lighting is fabulous. If you're recording straight onto your computer and running webinars and masterclasses—and being a course creator, as you are—then purchase one of these as soon as your budget allows.

$ $ $

When you're starting out, don't spend money you don't have to. Create the set you need for your audience and budget. If you're doing anything to do with cooking and filming in the kitchen, wear a lapel mic so you can walk around freely as you're doing it. If you're an accountant and you're talking about finance, you might be sitting behind your desk. If you're talking about presentation skills, then you're going to be standing up and walking around a little.

Take into account all these variables when creating your set. While it's tempting to go all out, you don't need to start off with the whole expensive production. One of the best things about starting your own online course business is how economical it is to do. Traditionally, going into business required an initial investment of tens of thousands of dollars; now you can get started with less than five thousand. And the money you put into starting your own digital empire could generate the best return on investment you'll ever make.

One of my past clients booked a studio for the day to record her course professionally. It cost her $4500. In that time she managed to finalise her welcome videos and one module with six lesson segments. The production quality was absolutely exceptional, but far from essential to begin with. The world needs you to launch. Keep it as economical and free of barriers as possible, recognising that you'll most likely be tweaking the first iteration of your course after your first round of students have gone through and given you feedback.

What we're here to do is deliver massive value to our students. Is having a super-fancy backdrop and 4K crisp filming going to make that learning experience any different? Probably not. It might be a little bit more aesthetically pleasing, but it won't affect the learning result.

Look at people you admire in the industry and what you love about their videos to decide what's important to you. I love Marie Forleo. She runs one of the best online programs in the world and is razor smart. Through her channel MarieTV she shares so much incredible information to help people entering the world of business. These videos have exceptional production quality, but then Marie has a massive budget. She does multimillion dollar launches. Don't compare the quality of your first videos to someone's ten thousandth.

One of my favourite things about Marie's videos is their entertainment value. I am fascinated by neuroscience and registered for further study in the area a couple of years ago with the aim of progressing my PhD. I lasted two whole months! While I loved the subject matter, I could not sit through the endless dry and boring lectures. The professor clearly knew his subject, but he made no attempt to engage let alone entertain his students. In some ways, it's even harder to teach people online than in person, because when online they're surrounded by far more distractions. They can pause you and switch you off with a click, whereas creeping out of a quiet lecture hall can be awkward and embarrassing.

Course creators are in the business of edutainment. You can have the greatest content in the world, but if it doesn't hold your audience's interest, it will never be shared as it deserves. This does not mean you need to be silly and dance around and be flamboyant, if that's not who you are. Edutainment means putting thought into what your audience will find interesting and entertaining, and doing whatever it takes to get the education part to land. As I've already noted, getting yourself into the right state of mind helps with this greatly. You need to show up as your best self. Focus on feeling happy, light, clear and calm and you'll totally nail it. Before you hit record, take a few deep breaths to centre yourself and focus, listen to great music and tell yourself how awesome you are. Then go!

Think of the best teachers you've had in your life, whether it was way back when you were at school or later on. What made those teachers memorable?

If you have a naturally monotonous style, don't put on an act and pretend to be this flamboyant extroverted human or it will be completely exhausting and you won't be able to show up consistently. It's important to be yourself, but an illuminated version of your best self.

Through your own particular human experience you have accumulated an incredible body of knowledge and expertise. It's your responsibility to share that knowledge with the world so you can make someone else's journey that bit easier and more joyful. The only person who will hold you back from sharing your expertise with the world is you. People will judge you no matter what, so forget about what other people say or think, because you'll never really know what that is or what's going on in their lives. Have fun sharing what's burning in you that you know will add value for others. Let your light shine to help others to shine brighter too.

Action steps

Record your practice welcome video.

Purchase your equipment.

Create your set.

09

Design your point of difference

You are your point of difference. That one sentence could stand as the whole chapter! Let me explain.

People think that if there's already a similar product in the market, they can't go there. Not so. If it's within your zone of genius, it's yours to own—in your own way. You are the secret sauce that will help your program stand out differently from others. People can copy what you do but they can't copy who you are.

I am copied all the time. For instance, in my high-level mastermind program, every 90 days we have a six-hour session in which we review the key areas in my clients' businesses to help them make strategic decisions and stay focused on their goals while not wasting time on what's not important. It's a big session and an important part of my program. Students of the 90-day planning sessions receive an accompanying workbook. A couple of months ago I discovered that one member of my program had downloaded all my resources and attempted to solicit my clients for their own business. They cut the header and footer off my planning document and inserted their own, then passed it off to their clients as their own work. A lot of course creators fear this sort of scenario, but I suggest it's not worth any time at all. It's going to happen to you eventually, and you can choose to pursue it legally or you can focus on moving on and being bigger and better.

The reason I share this story is that even though my planning booklet was copied and I spend six hours guiding students through it, I draw on my 16 years of business experience to answer people's questions, hot seat various members, ask challenging questions and inspire people to chase their dreams. The planning booklet is all kinds of awesome sauce, but it's not where the magic lies. The magic is within you.

When creating your course, don't aim to be all things to all people. Seek instead to be perfect for one, and when you are you will be speaking to others too. Messaging that is too general is not going to solve your client's specific problem. Being clear about your purpose and super specific about who you serve will help you to clarify and amplify your message.

When developing a course, pick one person to build it for. You're creating this course because you know there's a need for it. People are asking you for it. Who is asking you? Pick that person right now and create it for them. Talk directly to them. With every module you write, with every lesson you record and resource you produce, create it for them. I have a fictional perfect client. Her name is Alice Carrington. I know everything about Alice. Every single time I decide to create something, whether it's lesson content or marketing materials or Facebook lives, I ask myself, 'Is this what Alice wants and needs right now?' If not, I'll scrap it. It's so much easier to think of one rather than many. Our wants and needs vary so widely that if you try to please everyone you'll end up pleasing no one.

Be perfect for your Alice Carrington, otherwise known as your *client avatar*. I've always found that term a little impersonal, which is why I invented Alice Carrington.

It will always be tempting to aim for broader appeal. You may think that by being so specific and focused, you are cutting off a segment of the market. And it's true, you are. If you run around in circles trying to please everyone, you'll end up exhausted as well as less successful. When you know your niche intimately and cater directly to your perfect client, your message is so clear that people know exactly what you're about, what you stand for and who you serve. It means more people will buy from you and recommend you because they know who you are and what you do. It also becomes easier to create great partnerships with other businesses that aren't competitive but have that same customer base.

Your niche is your very own segment of the market. It is simply the perfect client in your segment. Among the unique niches I have seen developed by successful course creators are corset making, flower arch making, creating Excel spreadsheet formulas, organic beekeeping and beatboxing. You'll find there's an audience for pretty much whatever you're passionate about. The wonderful thing about the web is that it brings together people from around the world who share a passion.

We know that the primary purpose of our course is to solve someone's problem. Feeling like you're really doing so, enriching their life and making an impact makes it really easy to get out of bed in the morning. Think about who your perfect client is and complete the following table.

Your perfect client

Fictional (or actual) name	Alice Carrington
Age range	25–65
What specific problem are you solving for them?	Helping Alice to package her expertise and sell it globally through personal branding and content marketing.
What stage of life are they in?	Growth phase! Alice is ready to unshackle and step into the life she's always dreamed of.
What makes them feel happy?	A wholesome life filled with love, family, friends, nature and a beautiful, impactful business.
Why are you the right person to solve their problem?	With 17 years of business experience in various educational businesses, I can help Alice overcome roadblocks and find the smoothest path to success.
What do they do for work?	Run their empire!
What do they do in their spare time?	Whatever they want! 'You do you' is the mantra for Alice.
What social media do they consume?	Mainly Instagram, but still on Facebook and LinkedIn.
What are their favourite books?	A combination of personal development, mindfulness, business—and, of course, a good trashy novel.
What podcasts are their favourites?	Business with some personality. Alice has no time for fluff.
What is their number one goal right now?	To have more fun in business as her dreams come true.
What are their top values and what's most important to them in life?	Family Health Financial wealth Friends Living a meaningful life of her own design

Specificity helps both you and your client gain the clarity you need. What sounds clearer to you?

1. Option 1: business secrets

2. Option 2: the secret formula for creating a Google systems site for your business to help you achieve more in less time.

Option 2 is certainly more wordy and won't win any awards for the world's catchiest title, but it will attract more customers. This is because 'business secrets' is so broad and general that you don't know exactly what you'll be getting. If your problem relates to systems and lack of time in your business, then option 2 is going to be a winner for you.

Knowing your perfect client helps you to use the right language to speak directly to them so when you're sharing your course on social media, podcasts and all over town, it cuts through the noise and your Alice Carrington will turn around and say, 'Oh my gosh, that's me! That's exactly what I need right now!'

Maybe down the road you'll want to serve other avatars or client types. It doesn't matter. In fact it will make it so much easier if you nail this one for your first course. One course = one perfect client. Expand to others once you've reached your critical goal in your first program.

If someone is already doing the very thing you want to cover, that's okay. In fact, it's a good thing. It means your perfect client is out there and already looking for more information. You just need to follow your heart and do it better, do it differently, draw on your unique experiences and appeal to your own perfect client.

Knowing your perfect client's values and challenges will allow you to remove resistance through the sales process and create content that fulfils the transformation promise and gives your students their best chance of success. A client of mine, Lisa, teaches mums how to capture those treasured moments in their children's lives without needing to hire a professional photographer. What's the greatest challenge her clients face in achieving their goal? It actually has less to do with technical expertise than with getting their children to sit still long enough! Because Lisa knows this, she doesn't overlook it in her photography course. Strategies for helping children enjoy being photographed doesn't necessarily have anything to do with photography and wasn't something Lisa talked about in the sales process, but she knows it's a challenge for many mums, so dedicating a lesson to it helps them to achieve the desired result.

In my work, I teach people how to make and grow an online micro business. Rather than opening it to everyone, I am especially passionate about helping women create online courses so they can work from home, build more wealth and enjoy more freedom in their lives. In saying that, I work with men all the time too. All types of people sign on to my course who are nothing like Alice Carrington. But by talking to Alice, I can really focus my language and content to make it perfect for her, while knowing it will still reach others who seek the same transformation result.

I'm writing this book for you. I know you value wealth and want to create a lot of it, but more than anything you value time and freedom. Having more money would be fabulous, but not at the cost of being chained to a desk 12 hours a day. The people I create for want to live life on their own terms, to live a life that matters. You know money buys freedom, and running online educational programs is one way to create wealth for yourself, your family and your community while enjoying freedom of choice in how you live.

Once you know your clients' values, you can assess their challenges. What is the problem they want help with? What is the hardest part of the problem they're trying to solve? Then, what will stop your perfect client from saying yes to your solution? Look at this as pragmatically and objectively as possible. If you look at everything you've created so far purely from the client's point of view, where are the holes? Are they turned off by the cost of the course? Is it that they don't have enough time to devote to the course?

If the transformation promise is actually fulfilled, it will mean a radical life change, which itself could hold them back from committing to it. Moving to a new level or new belief often means leaving old, familiar ones behind, and that can be uncomfortable and scary. Although your client wants what you've got, if the program is going to be life altering, you will experience resistance and will need to allow for that so you can mitigate those objections and gently guide people towards their desired goal.

Action step

Create your 'perfect' client.

10
Design your brand and what you stand for

Defining your brand and bringing it to life is one of the most exciting parts of your journey. I love the aesthetics and the branding. I opened the doors of my first business when I was 20. The day my business cards arrived and I sat them on the front counter and stood back and looked at them, I felt so proud. It's an incredible feeling to see something you've imagined and dreamed of come to life before your eyes. Before you know it, what has been no more than a dream in your heart will become tangibly real right in front of you.

Your brand is not just your logo. Rather, it encompasses everything in the marketplace that allows your customers to perceive and interpret your business. In this chapter we'll look at your logo, touching on colours and fonts. I'll discuss how to begin setting all this up and how to get started on social media so you're familiar and confident when it's time to launch. At the end of this chapter, if you want to go old school and have some business cards printed, you can order those beautiful pieces of card that symbolise your new business.

To establish brand recognition, your branding needs to be consistently visible through everything you produce. When someone scrolls through Instagram or checks out a workbook of yours or spots your sticker on the back of a client's laptop, what they see needs to be recognisably yours and to embody all the qualities you want to be known for. Even your tone of voice and the clothes you wear can play a part in your brand.

Start with this exercise: Think about everything you want your brand to represent. Do you want a rich, luxe look? A fresh look? Bright colours or black and white? High end or high volume? Strong or soft? Do you want to be known for fun or for seriousness? Do you want to project comfort and approachability or exclusivity?

Once you have refined the feel you want to create, it's much easier to move on to the tangible aspects of branding.

Designing your logo

I love logo design! I know I've said that already, but branding is just so much fun. It's the outward expression of everything you do. You need to put a lot of thought and effort into your logo design because it's going to be everywhere, and although you can change it, you definitely don't want to do so often as it's a lot of work but, more importantly, you'll lose brand recognition.

A logo is part of your brand. You need to absolutely love your logo and what it means to you. This doesn't mean it has to be super elaborate or complex. Look at some of the most well-known logos in the world such as those of Apple, Nike and Google. They're not at all elaborate, but they're universally recognised.

Your logo may incorporate your name (if you're building a business on your personal brand) or your company name. It may be based on words or incorporate a mark or image. To get a feel for what you like, do a simple Google image search. If you want a fun logo, search 'fun logo' and scroll through what comes up. When you see something that appeals to you, save it and record what you like about it and what you don't. Collect at least 10 examples of logo styles and elements you love before progressing to the design stage. If you're getting a graphic designer to design a logo for you, this will make the process much cheaper and faster as you can be really clear and concise in your instructions. You'll be a dream to work with because your designer will have a much better idea of what you want.

Producing those first few variations can be incredibly exciting and you'll be tempted to share them with the world to ask for feedback on which of them people like best. I urge you to resist this temptation, as everyone will have a different opinion and you'll be left unsure and worried about which way to go. Trust your own responses and intuition. You'll immediately know whether it's a 'Hell yes! That's me!' or you need something different. Go with what *you* love, because it's you who will be living and working with it constantly. If I want constructive feedback, I have a circle of trusted business friends who will give me specific and helpful feedback. If you ask your uncle who knows nothing of design or marketing, then his feedback—'I don't like the colour' or 'looks too simple'—is likely to be absolutely useless to you.

Settle on a logo that you'll be proud to have around you and be associated with for years to come. Here are just four options for logo creation worth considering, depending on your budget:

Canva

I'll talk more about Canva later. It's one of my favourite pieces of software ever! Canva makes graphic design super simple. They have logo samples and templates within the program so you can choose what you like, mix and match, and customise to your colours and fonts.

Fiverr

Fiverr is an online marketplace of freelancers across the globe. Whenever you need something designed, you can connect with someone who'll make it happen. A great logo may cost between $10 and $100. Sometimes you get what you pay for. The most successful way to use Fiverr is to restrict your searches to freelancers with a five-star rating who have done a lot of work on the platform and built a solid reputation.

Creative Market

Creative Market is a wonderland for course creators. It's filled with logos, templates and digital goodies for everything you never knew you needed in your business. Browse 'logos' and you'll soon find something you love. Then you can either tweak it yourself to add your colours, font and feel, or give it to a designer on Fiverr to turn your idea into reality.

A graphic designer

A qualified designer will often charge around $1000 for a logo design package that includes creating a brand board for you and logo variations and revisions. While pricier, it's worth spending the money if you don't have any design skills or you're not completely clear on what you want, as they'll provide you with options you've never thought of and have ninja creative skills.

Colours and fonts

I have known people to disappear down the rabbit hole of colour and font variations for days! It's very easy at this stage to get analysis paralysis and become overwhelmed by all the options. This is where your intuition becomes invaluable. Make a considered decision here, but don't overthink it. When you see something you love, try it on for size then lock it in and move on.

Colours and fonts are important, though. Decide on one primary colour and two to five secondary colours, depending on your brand feel.

Even people who go with black and white will add a pop of accent colour every now and then when they need to.

To get your creative juices flowing use colour picker tools. For example:

- **Complimentary colour options:** www.paletton.com

- **Trending colour palettes:** www.coolors.co/palettes

- **Colour picking tool:** www.canva.com/colors/color-wheel/

- **Colour combinations:** www.canva.com/ learn/100-color-combinations

Sometimes you'll really love a colour scheme but it doesn't suit what you're trying to project. Think about your client, your values and the look and feel you want to create with your brand, and focus on colours you love and gravitate towards that can convey that. Once you've settled on your colours, record their hex codes. That's what you'll need for your website and design.

With your logo, you can go nuts with the font and do whatever you like as it will be locked in the image. With your brand fonts, though, don't get too elaborate as you don't want to have to embed custom code on a website. Better to keep it as simple and clean as possible so it's easy for customers to read.

Choose three fonts:

- **Heading font.** This will be the heading on your website, your social posts, webinars and workbooks. *Hot tip:* As pretty as some script fonts are, keep your heading clean and easy to read.

- **Body font.** This font will be used for the bulk of the text on your website, so again it must be super easy to read.

- **Accent font.** This is where you can get more creative. Your accent font is for your labels and any words you want to pop.

If you're building your website on a platform such as Kajabi, check their available fonts. You can always import a custom font, but it will fail on some internet browsers, so rather than run the risk of your beautiful, carefully chosen font showing up as Times New Roman (eek!), choose one that is coded into the software.

Once you have your logo, colours and fonts settled, you'll want to create a brand board as a resource you can refer to whenever you create something new so you maintain consistency. It's also a helpful resource to provide to any freelancers you engage to help you with your marketing.

A basic brand board includes:

- logo

- logo variations (maybe you have horizontal and vertical versions or an alternate colour depending on background)

- fonts

- colour palette

- image samples

- background images

- mission and transformation promise

- elements.

Curious experimenting

I've added curious experimenting here because I know when you get to this stage a lot of what we're doing can feel very permanent. You might think, 'Oh, hang on a minute, what if I want to change my mind? What if I don't want to keep it like that?' That's okay. Where possible, you don't want to change your business name, and you don't want to change your logo without making a big deal of your rebrand so your customers continue to know who you are. Keep the colours as consistent as possible, especially your main colour.

But you can tweak and experiment to your heart's content the entire way through the journey until you hit go, then don't obsess over the details, know that it's done and move on.

Landing page

A landing page is simply a page on your website that invites a customer to take the next step with you. Sometimes that could be downloading a resource you've created, sometimes it's signing up to your webinar, sometimes a sale. A typical landing page conversion rate is around 1.5 per cent. That means 1.5 per cent of clicks that open this page will take the next step. I say 1.5 per cent of 'clicks' and not 'people' because often one person will go to your website several times before they take the next step with you.

Either way, 1.5 per cent sounds really low, but small tweaks can make a big difference. When you first start and you put everything out there, people will come straight to your website and check you out.

You can then look at the conversion rate of each page and each ad, and get a sense of what worked well and what didn't. A little tweak can then lift the conversion from 1.5 to, say, 1.75 per cent. Constant small improvements across all areas of your business can make a big difference to your bottom line. As you continue on your online business journey, you'll find it often comes down to being open to accepting that you're going to do things before you feel completely ready. You'll do things before you're completely sure of what you're doing. Accept that there's room for improvement and commit to continuous improvement as you progress.

Often I see clients stagnate for far too long because they don't want to launch without feeling like everything is perfect. Perfection, as I've already argued, is illusory. You can never feel completely ready to do something you've never done before. Progress beats perfection every single day. People who sit on their online course idea for years because it doesn't yet feel perfect are steadily overtaken by others who are prepared to take imperfect action. You turn your dreams into reality by making a plan of action steps, implementing each one, and continuing to evolve and improve as you gain more skills. Knowledge means nothing without action.

The world is changing so quickly, the customer's needs are changing so quickly, the market is changing so quickly that you need to stay agile and continue to change along with it. Adopt a strategy of constant curious experimenting. Instead of looking at your business as either going well or going badly, think, 'Ah, that's interesting'. Keep an open mind, make frequent adjustments and gauge the results so you can constantly do better. Let it flow and live and evolve as you and your clients do.

Social media

People have very different views of social media usage. I myself have a love–hate relationship with it, knowing the damage it can do. But if you want to run a business, you can't afford not to have a social media presence.

Instagram

Instagram—like all social media, for that matter—is constantly changing, so I won't offer step-by-step instructions. Want to know how I learned what to do in all aspects of my business? I googled stuff. Google and YouTube are my best friends. Okay, that sounds a little sad, but really there's nothing they don't know! Whatever I want to do, I type it in and some wonderful human somewhere has created practical instructions and uploaded them onto the internet.

Create your Instagram profile using your personal or company name, whichever you decided to run with for your brand. Social media is *social*, so you'll often find quicker success using a personal name than a business name. If you're unsure how to do it, type 'How to start an

Instagram account' into YouTube and you'll have your instructions in a matter of seconds.

Facebook

I think every business should have an Instagram and a Facebook page. Why make life harder for yourself than it has to be? Embrace social media and the superpowers it can provide for your business.

Creating your Facebook page

If you're one of the 2.7 billion people on the planet who currently have a personal Facebook account, you now need to create a business page for your new digital course business.

Use Facebook to its full potential. Include your profile image, cover photo, bio and list of services, and your call to action button on your cover photo. Ensure you fill in every field so you can take advantage of all the opportunities offered. Then share it with the world!

Creating a Facebook group

Once you've created your Facebook page, if you decided to host your members-only group on Facebook and not inside Kajabi's Community product, go ahead and create that now. Facebook groups are a great way to engage your community, but they're also a lot of work. In each group you want to keep members active, which means *you* have to be active within the group. So don't start too many different ones at the beginning or you'll spend all day in there.

I've seen start-ups do a Facebook page, a members-only group and a group for non-members. This can work very well, but go in with your eyes wide open, knowing it's going to take a lot of effort. To begin with, I recommend launching with just a members-only group until you get the hang of everything and can consistently deliver great quality content and encourage engagement within your group.

The upside of having a closed Facebook group that's available to non-paying members is that you can include people who are engaging with your work but are not quite ready to take the leap into becoming a paying customer. You can build a relationship with your potential customers more easily within a Facebook group than from your public Facebook page. Think of the Facebook page as the front door. Your non-members Facebook group welcomes people into your lounge room; your members get to wander through the rest of the house. The non-member Facebook group also acts as a lead-generating tool. When people ask to join a group, you can request their email address and add them to your marketing list. Your email list will often convert potential customers into paying customers at a much higher rate than social media, so this is a valuable asset to collect.

LinkedIn

Depending on your business, you may want to create a company page on LinkedIn. For professional services it's important to have a presence on LinkedIn. In most cases, whether or not it's going to be an active channel for you, it's worth setting up a presence on all the main social media channels, so you can hold that space for your brand and ensure you're prepared for any changes in functionality and popularity down the track.

Twitter

Go where your customers are. If none of them are on Twitter, then it's not worth spending your time marketing on Twitter, but it is worth setting up your username just in case. For most businesses, Facebook and Instagram are where their customers are.

Other social media

Don't spend all your time posting on different social networks, but if your customers are there, then it's definitely worth jumping on. Look at where your customers are and what they enjoy engaging in, and work out how you can be great at that.

Blog posts

Blogging was all the rage in the early days of online marketing. Some activities stand the test of time. Internet search is going to be such a beautiful friend to you, so you want to do everything you can to make it as simple as possible for your perfect clients to find you. And blogging is going to help this so much.

Depending on your writing skills, writing a blog post could be a simple 10-minute exercise or it could take you a day of agonising research and procrastination. Choose to make life easy for yourself and remember that done is better than perfect.

Today we are bombarded with information constantly. So much content is getting banged out that even the biggest newspapers in the world are putting them out with typos in them and without fact checking. I'm not saying you should do the same, but a blog post is not held to the same standard as a university-level essay.

The most popular blog posts consist of a really short, digestible piece of information that adds value to your customer's day. It may not change their life, but it could be a piece of information they have been searching for, something that could help them right now. It will also demonstrate that you have the skills to deliver this information for them.

Then, at the end of your gorgeously helpful blog post, you can invite the reader to take the next step with you. Sometimes that's as simple as asking them to subscribe so you can build that all-important email marketing list; sometimes it's offering them a more enticing resource that you know would be a good next step for them in exchange for their email address.

My absolute favourite blog in the world is written by Seth Godin. He posts every single day, and they're tiny in terms of word count but massively impactful and thought provoking. It shows you don't need to rattle on and on to make a difference with your posts.

A good format to follow when getting started on blog writing is to write an introduction of a few sentences, some dot points for your main ideas then a few sentences to sum up. Around half a standard page is a good length to aim for to get a feel for writing blog posts. If it takes you more than 30 to 60 minutes to write, you're wasting your time. An easy prompt for knowing what to write is when a client asks a question. I have an ideas folder on a Monday.com board (more about that software in chapter 17), then whenever I'm asked a question or have a new idea, I'll add it to my ideas board. When it comes time to write content, I can go through my ideas and work out what to use for a podcast episode, a blog post and a social media post.

Collect a bank of a few blog posts so as soon as your website goes live you have some information there to start growing. Then choose whether you'll post weekly, monthly or at some other regular interval to continue to add more content.

Posting a regular blog benefits your SEO (Search Engine Optimisation) in a Google search directly. You can also share your posts on other sites and link back to your own website, which in turn will also increase your SEO.

If you're not a fan of writing, that shouldn't stop you from publishing articles on your blog. Use a software package such as Otter.ai to transcribe your speech so you just need to do some light editing and add it in. I find that while driving my thoughts run free and I often get great content ideas. I ask my phone to create a voice recording and just start speaking. I then upload the recording into Otter.ai and bang, I have my blog post. Otter is a voice-to-text software I tell you more about in chapter 17. When you find it difficult to do something you need to do to help your business to grow, know that there's always an easier way—you just need to find it.

Branding is your face to the world and what potential customers will first judge you on, so create a brand you're proud of and get it out there.

Action steps

Design your logo.

Settle on your colour palette.

Choose your three fonts.

Set up your social media profiles.

Write a blog post.

11

Nail your first offer and program

My goal for you is that by the time you have completed the last chapter of this book you'll know exactly what your first course is going to be and will be ready to launch it out into the world. Your first signature program will draw on what you're best at. You have already established what that is. Now we're going to package it into a saleable product and price it. If it hasn't already, impostor syndrome may arise here. In this chapter we'll attempt to put a value on the knowledge you have and the results you can achieve for people, and that will bring up all kinds of psychological issues.

I wrote a lot about impostor syndrome in my last book, *One Life*, so I won't go into detail here, other than to note that it can be a major obstacle to turning your dreams into reality. Every businessperson is a salesperson. You have to sell your products to make money, and when *you* are the product it can feel a lot more personal than it actually is. Invest time in books and programs that can help you to push past feelings of self-doubt and work on your mindset, so you can help yourself rather than holding yourself back. Many external factors can contribute to frustrating your efforts, but more often than not mindset issues and self-sabotage play a role. No one is immune to it. Every time you level up in your business, you will be presented with a new mental barrier to overcome.

Launching one course is a very manageable goal. If you focus on just doing this one thing to the best of your ability, you will experience much earlier success and be able to build your confidence. Doing a brilliant job on one course will build your momentum, moving you forward towards introducing more courses to your stoked and growing client base.

We know that if you're an expert in social media you'd achieve greater success running a course on 'Facebook 101: Starting your Facebook business journey' than on 'Social media success', because specificity and clarity win. Your goal with your first program is to bridge your clients' knowledge gap. To do this, we'll look at the learning bridge we need to design to move them from Point A to Point B.

Back yourself

We've already settled on your course name and course outline so I don't want to throw a spanner in the works, but I want to ensure you're as certain as you can be before launch. Too often I find people doubt their expertise and question whether they're good enough to teach others. Dan told me he had over a decade of experience teaching others how to invest in real estate. He was passionate about it, but he still worried he would be picked apart because he didn't have a university qualification in it. There will always be people who know more than you and people who know less than you. You need to be totally confident in your ability to help your students to achieve their goal. Does that mean you have to be the best in the world at it? No. But you must be able to say, 'I can add massive value to these people's lives. And I can bridge that gap from point A to point B, and fulfil every promise I've made in this course'. Dan could package his knowledge and expertise with the practical experience he'd acquired over the past decade.

Very occasionally I encounter the flip side of this mindset. A man in one of my business groups—let's call him Bob—boasted about how he'd just made $10000 on the launch of his first course, which aimed to help newly divorced dads talk to their children through the separation and to find the new normal. As Bob answered other group members' questions it emerged that he had never married, had no children and had no professional qualifications or experience in mental health or counselling. He did have a lot of experience in Facebook advertising, though. He found that this was something people were very concerned about, and he decided it would cost very little to sell them into a course on this subject. So after a few days' online research he put together his course, and people started buying it. He was stoked. Ew!

Don't be like Bob. He'll be found out real fast and suffer massive reputational damage, as he deserves. Play the long game and serve people brilliantly. I know from the thousands of people I've worked with on online courses that Bob's story is a rare one. Actually, Bob's is the only example I've ever witnessed. As I've said, it's far more common to find that self-doubt is what's holding people back. You have amazing information inside that beautiful brain of yours. Unlock the magic and spread it out into the world.

I spoke earlier about competition. Now it's getting real, so I want to go deeper. It doesn't matter that someone is already offering a course similar to yours. Competition is great, because it means there is already a market for your course. No one else in the world has your personality, your unique life experience or your communication style. You could be exactly what someone out there is waiting for right now to get them from where they are to where they want to be. Each person is attracted to a different sort of learning delivery, and your unique style and offering could be just what that person is looking for. I know it frustrates Mat no end when I do something that someone else has taught me when he's been telling me to do it for years! I have never been a slim girl and I have a frustratingly slow metabolism, so I have to be very conscious of what I eat. Mat is an exceptionally healthy man. For 18 years he has been telling me I just need to eat loads of vegetables and no sugar, and to move my body for 30 minutes every day. Then last year I took a course called Fast 800, run by TV journalist and author Dr Michael Mosley, and my body loved it. It obviously covers more than this, but basically it comes down to eating loads of healthy, organic, non-starchy vegetables, good protein, no sugar—and moving your body! I couldn't hear the message in the same way from Mat as I did from the course. To bring about any form of personal transformation, you need to receive the information from the right person at the right time or it will likely fall on deaf ears. This is why it's so vital to be yourself, so you can attract the right people.

By letting your own light shine, you will naturally attract your tribe. It will set you apart from your competitors, because you're not trying to be like anyone else. You're different, which means competition actually doesn't matter. While it's good to be aware of it, I'm not big on paying too much attention to what the competition is doing. Make sure you're running your own race, playing your own game.

If you spend too much time checking out everyone else, you'll wind up adopting some of the thinking you need to change, which will affect your performance and dilute your awesomeness. You'll start to second guess yourself and be pulled in different directions, and you'll lose your focus. Don't stalk your competitors' Instagram pages, even just to check how much engagement they have on their social posts—I know you've been there! It's bad for your mental health. Do things your way and fill the needs and gaps you can see in your market.

Most Australians don't like to toot their own horn. Self-deprecation is generally seen as an admirable trait, but it will not serve you well when you're trying to create a successful business. Interestingly, most of my American clients haven't heard of 'Tall Poppy Syndrome', which is so prevalent in Australia.

To position yourself as a thought leader and go-to expert in your industry, you need to stand tall, to be that tall poppy. If you're holding yourself back for fear of how others may judge you, ask yourself, 'Is this helpful?' Does playing small help you or the world? It may be comfortable but it certainly isn't useful and won't be conducive to creating a beautiful, fulfilled life.

I'm a big personal development fan. I once attended a seminar weekend run by Dr John Demartini in which he instructed us to write down 100 things we love about ourselves. That was hard. We're often far more critical than complimentary about ourselves, which is ridiculous! You're the one you're with all the time. Support yourself. You might like to have a go at that exercise but if not, answer the following questions so you can prove to yourself that you're 'worthy' enough to package and sell your expertise:

- Do you know what you're talking about?

- What experiences have you had that give you the credibility to teach this content?

- Are there other people out there currently teaching a similar course who are less qualified and experienced than you?

- What skills do you have in this area that qualify you to deliver the course?

- Why would someone recommend you to a friend interested in your subject?

- If someone were to recommend you, what would you hope they'd say?

- Why would someone buy from you?

- What makes you unique?

No one else has exactly the same traits and gifts as you. Recognise your own personal blend of awesomeness and put it out into the world.

Your magnetic offer framework

It's time to talk about your offer. This is the package and value you'll deliver through helping people achieve the result they want. Remember that it's all a curious experiment, so you may not nail your value proposition first time. Your value proposition is what inclusions and value you're offering in exchange for the price you've set. Once you launch, it's highly likely you'll want to make adjustments going forward, and that's totally fine.

For your first course, keep it simple. Don't start with something too elaborate and cumbersome with too many moving parts. The hardest part of a launch is actually letting go and ripping off that bandaid. While it's all still conceptual you feel safe, but as one of my favourite observations from John A. Shedd goes, 'A ship in harbour is safe, but that's not what ships are built for'.

Your offer is designed to attract your perfect client like a magnet. As soon as they see or hear it they'll be pulled in, because it's just the force they need in their life right now.

The simplest way to launch your course offer is to establish two pricing options: one to pay upfront and one to pay in instalments. Complete the following table. I explain next how to determine each of the parts we haven't already looked at.

Your magnetic offer

Course name	Limited Launch Formula
The problem it solves	Walks course creators through step by step of the live 8-day launch process, showing the theory, marketing and tech.
Who it's for	Course creators who have everything ready to go and now need to sell it to the world with a proven system to follow.

Transformation promise	How to do an 8-day OpenCart launch formula on Kajabi that gets results.
Course length	12 weeks, self-paced
Access duration	12 months
Course delivery	Combination of Zoom, Loom and face to camera
Inclusions	Pre-recorded lessons Site map for launch Launch checklist Launch email copy Launch Canva templates Webinar checklist Webinar site map
Course price	$297
Instalments price	4 x $89 payments
Launch bonus	Live Q&A session
Upsell	Add Personal Brand Builder
Graduate's next step	Join Her Empire Builder mastermind

Transformation promise

This is what people are buying: the result you can provide through the transformation.

This course will take people from _____
to _____ in _____ by _____
_____

For example:

My course takes people from **complete novice** to **running a sustainable organic backyard vegetable patch** in **12 weeks** by **providing you with the theoretical and practical knowledge and skills you need.**

Course length

In the world of online courses, the length of the course is often only conceptual. It gives people a guide to how the course is divided into parts so they can stage themselves through the program. Depending on access and delivery, and their own time constraints, people will rarely complete your course according to the timeline you initially set. When deciding on your course length, make it achievable and appealing. While they're essentially the same, for some in your audience a 30-day challenge, with content dripped through daily, may seem more attractive than a four-week course that releases content weekly.

Your first course may be so content heavy that the only way it could be achieved by your clients is if you make it a 12-month course. If that's where you are right now, I encourage you to break it up and start with a simple 4- to 12-week course so people can get to know you as a course creator without needing to commit too much time and money. Once they've completed your first course, you can encourage them to sign up for the big kahuna.

Access duration

We spoke about this earlier in the book. This is how long from the time of purchase you're going to grant your clients access. Longer shouldn't be mistaken for more valuable. Allow enough time that you know your perfect client can get it all done, then add a little more before cutting it off so you can encourage completion of the course.

Course delivery

This is about whether you decide to drip-feed content or release it all so students can self-pace. Content can be set to start on a certain date. You'll also decide whether to live teach or pre-record all modules.

Inclusions

Here you can spell out the inclusions in your course to build your value proposition. When deciding on your offer inclusions, you can choose what to include from the following offer menu:

- pre-recorded instructional videos

- live webinars (number of)

- group coaching calls (number of)

- one-to-one coaching calls (number of)

- checklists

- templates

- specific resources

- priority email access

- live event tickets

- members-only community page.

Course price

Setting the price for your online course can be tricky. Back when I owned my retail store, we would buy a product for $2 and sell it for $4. It was all very straightforward, with only small variations to this equation. When pricing your online course, you will take into account:

- the value you're providing

- the cost to deliver

- your growth strategy and market positioning

- what your customer is willing to pay

- how much money you want to make.

The value you're providing

Calculating the value you're providing can be easier when people are making money from your course. Rachel teaches a course on how to create flower arches for weddings, which is a massive money-maker for florists and demands a specific skill set that's in hot demand. Each flower arch will sell for around $2000. Rachel has priced her course at $2499, because she knows that after a florist has used the skills she has taught them just twice, they've already covered their return on investment and can continue to bring in revenue for their business.

For Renee it's a little harder. She teaches women who have always had a desire to play the piano to pick up a song in 12 weeks. At the completion of Renee's course, you're not going to be able to (or want to) go out and perform and make money from it, so the value of the course doesn't have a financial return attached to it. This is true of many online course products and is where you must draw on other factors to help you determine your pricing.

The cost to deliver

In our budgeting section, we included a brief overview of the expenses of running an online course business. As with every business, these will vary depending on your habits and, especially, your marketing strategy. When you look at the cost of delivering your course, you need to focus on the direct cost.

If you're going to mail out a welcome pack that costs you $100, then you need to take account of this. You're looking at your time as a cost of delivering the course. If you've set up a pre-recorded course and you're not including any live teaching components, then it's completely scalable—that is, it won't cost you more to run the program for 1000 people than it does to run it for 100 people. If you're bringing in guest experts and paying them to live teach in your course, you'll also factor that cost into your pricing.

Growth strategy and market positioning

Your growth strategy and market positioning are major considerations when determining your pricing. I've found that people have the most success when they pick their positioning strategy and stick with it. The two main strategies are low-cost, low-touchpoint and high-volume courses versus high-cost, high-touchpoint and low-volume courses. The perception of a $29 course is very different from that of a $290 course or a $2900 course. If you go low cost, then you're going to need to sell *a lot* of courses, and the easiest way to do that is by spending a bucketload of money on social media advertising.

It may be tempting to price lower, thinking it will bring more sales, but it's often easier to make a $200 sale than a $20 sale, because people don't think they'll get much of value for $20. They probably purchased from an ad on a whim, and the chances of their completing the course, or even opening the package, are very low. No one ever wins by being the cheapest in the market.

You can probably tell I prefer the high-cost, low-volume strategy. The higher the cost, the greater the expectation and the more the touchpoints, so you need to ensure you can deliver the value.

What your customer is willing to pay

This is the final component we look at when price setting. I've seen a course creator charge $45000 for his year-long course. Because he has a stellar reputation, and places in his course are limited, there's scarcity involved, so he has been able to continually raise the price and his customers are happy to pay it to be part of his program.

Know your worth and your value. Don't undercut yourself and your talents. Always offer exceptional value, but don't feel like you can't charge what you're worth. You will always have people tell you your prices are too high (if you don't, you need to raise your prices!). When this happens it doesn't mean your course is actually too expensive; it just means it's too expensive for that particular customer at that time, or you haven't communicated the value you offer clearly enough.

Go for quality over price every time. This is where it comes back to playing the long game. If you focus on creating a quality product that you can charge a premium price for, and you consistently deliver value, month after month, year after year, then your credibility and reputation for integrity will grow too and you'll soon hit the magic million. You may start out a bit slower, because you're growing through value-based marketing rather than advertising, but in three years' time you'll be light years ahead of where you would have been if you had kept it cheap and nasty.

How much money do you want to make?

Work out your income goal and calculate backwards from there. If your first-year goal is to make $10000 a month, and you're going to charge $1000 for your course, you'll need only 10 customers per month, which should be pretty achievable, depending on your market.

If, conversely, you're charging $99 for your course, you're going to need 101 customers a month to make the same money. Play around with your course prices and look at how many sales you would need to make to achieve your income goal.

Figure 2 shows the different sales you would need to close in order to make a million dollars a year. I know, everything looks easier on paper, but it's so achievable!

Instalments price

If your course is priced at over $100, then offering an instalment option removes affordability as a barrier to taking your course. When you include an instalment option you're essentially acting like a bank, and carrying a risk on future payments, so you'll charge more, usually adding around 10 to 20 per cent to the total course price. For example, you might set an upfront course price of $997 with an option of paying six monthly instalments of $197.

How to make $1 million in a year

5000 people	buy a $200 product or pay $17 per month on membership
2000 people	buy a $500 product or pay $42 per month on membership
1000 people	buy a $1000 product or pay $83 per month on membership
500 people	buy a $2000 product or pay $167 per month on membership
300 people	buy a $3333 product or pay $278 per month on membership
100 people	buy a $10 000 product or pay $833 per month on membership

$1 000 000

Figure 2: The path to that first million

Launch bonus

A launch bonus is a step above a freebie, something with good perceived value but that's not necessarily worth buying on its own. It's designed to add value to the offer and help to pull people who are resisting your offer over the line. Design your bonuses to address objections. For example, if you're running a course on how to develop confidence on camera, a bonus could be something you know will address the anxiety some people have around showing up on camera. This might be a personal stylist's guide to nailing your on-camera look or a five-minute meditation to listen to just before you hit record. Other examples are a mini course, a guidebook or a group coaching call.

A launch bonus is offered for a limited time. You may offer it to people who sign up in the first 24 hours, so you're encouraging sales as soon as you open your cart. Or you could offer a bonus within a certain time frame after you run your sales webinar. A bonus is a way to create scarcity and provide an incentive that encourages people to stop thinking about it and move into action.

Upsell

This is definitely not an essential for your first course, but it may be something to consider if you have a product component or want to offer an upgrade. Say you're running a course on how to convert to a plant-based diet. Once people go through the checkout, you can have a pop-up upsell option offering them the option of adding a cookbook or cooking utensils that you also sell. Those who run courses that involve no individual touchpoints could offer the upgrade of a one-to-one call.

Graduate's next step

I recommend you don't lock in your next steps until you've put your first group through your course. By then you'll be able to identify any holes in your course and revise it accordingly, and you'll also know exactly where your clients want to progress to next, because they'll tell you. The easiest path to success is to give people what they're asking you for.

If you kick off your micro business with an eight-week course, then at around the six-week mark you can start talking about the next linear step in the customers' journey, and your next offer, so when they finish they can continue on their journey with you.

Your launch offer

Your first launch may be a big public event, or you may do a smaller, softer launch, sometimes called a 'beta launch'. In your beta launch you're very upfront, telling your clients that you're new to this and want lots of feedback as they move through your course. It's a paid trial for your clients, but at a special discounted introductory rate.

If you're more comfortable with the idea of launching to a beta group than to the public, individually invite current clients or people you know who might benefit from the course, people you can rely on to give you honest feedback. Then you can ask them all about their experience as a customer.

Action step

Create your magnetic offer.

SUCCESS STORY

Kayse Morris
The CEO Teacher

Kayse is a former teacher who started selling her teaching resources online back in 2013. After a few years of decent success, other teachers started to ask her about how they could do what she does and sell their teaching resources online full time. Today, Kayse runs a seven-figure business changing the lives of teachers and students all over the world through The CEO Teacher.

I caught up with Kayse in December 2020.

How you did you move from teaching into this online world?

I think we've got to go back to when I started my job as a teacher. For eight years, I taught middle school English and language arts. I began my journey teaching sixth grade for three years, and then moved to my sweet spot of teaching eighth grade. To be honest, I loved my job when I finally decided to leave the classroom. But it wasn't always like that, because when I finished college and started my career as a teacher, I thought it was going to be easy. I thought it was going to give me everything that life had to offer. Unfortunately, I was really struggling to come up with content for my classes while also being a full-time mom because, I didn't realise it at the time, for four long and agonizing years I struggled through a deep postpartum depression.

135

Dealing with all of that, I often found I didn't have the energy to write my own lesson plans, so I would search the internet every morning for help and that's when I stumbled on this website called Teachers Pay Teachers. It's an online marketplace where teachers buy and sell their resources to each other. The teachers I was buying from had no idea they were helping me get through some of the darkest days of my life. I no longer had to write those lesson plans—everything was already laid out for me. As crazy as it sounds, with that, I found my joy in teaching again, and I started to relate more to my students. That went on for about six months.

During that time, I also went to my doctor and said something I should have years earlier. When doctors ask postpartum moms questions like 'Are you sad?' or 'Do you cry for no reason?', I finally answered yes and said, 'Hey, I think I need help. I'm really struggling and can't do this alone'. That moment, in conjunction with the moment I told my husband that I thought I could start selling my resources online, will go down in history as my 'me moment' of all time.

I started as a teacher in the classroom and began selling my resources online in October 2013. From there it just grew. My first month I made $50. And I wanted to pay our Netflix bill, which at that time was $8.99, because we were gonna have to cut that out of the budget. My husband's now a high-school principal, but at that time he was teaching as well. So I made $50. I was on top of the world. Finally, I was getting paid for my performance. It felt like, you know, the more effort I put in, the more money I made.

That's exactly why I left teaching.

You get it. So you put in double the effort of the teacher next to you, yet you still earn the same pay cheque.

Yes, 100 per cent.

Then it turned into what it is today. The first year I made like $6000 and I thought that was amazing. Then I made my teaching salary, then

I tripled my teaching salary—all while I was still in the classroom. In 2017 I decided to leave the classroom to pursue this passion full time.

In November 2018 I launched my very first online course, which taught teachers how to do it too, because the number one question I was asked was, 'You quit teaching … you guys must be struggling?' I was helping people at night, teachers in my hometown. I decided to launch my own course and the rest is history.

You did $6000 in the first year. At what point did you go, 'Hold on, I think this may be like a real thing for me and not just covering the Netflix bill'?

I think by year three I was really in my stride. I had started perfecting systems and processes. There were people who had been doing it for six years before me. One of them—she was the very first millionaire on Teachers Pay Teachers—was featured in all of these articles and I printed them out and put them up on my board and I was like, oh my gosh, this is a possibility. But I was struggling to find my grounding, because these people had been doing it for years and I felt like I was always trying to catch up. So I had to find the ace in the hole, or what I like to call my Willy Wonka golden ticket. I had to figure out what I could learn that would give me a bit of an advantage. It turned out to be search engine optimisation, and that's a trick I teach all my students today.

So you tripled your salary before you decided to leave teaching?

I had actually made $100000 that year in addition to my teaching salary, just selling my resources online.

Wow. Did you feel like you had to go above and beyond before you were safe to leave your job?

Yeah, and it tugged on our heartstrings a lot. I loved those kids. I actually quit one year and then asked for my job back. Because uncertainty is hard, you know—to go out into the great unknown and to leave these kids. And I felt like I was making a difference in their lives. I don't know that I ever felt great about it. You know, I had all of my eggs in one basket. And that is a very scary thing. That was when I left and this became my full-time income. I knew that if I wanted to sleep at night, I had to diversify my income. So that's when I looked into courses.

So how did that first course go? Were you uber successful right out of the gate?

I was so blessed. It's so fun to go back there. Because it was just two years ago. I was seven months pregnant when I launched my first course. When I'm pregnant, I'm in like go mode. I'm pregnant again with number five. So it's like the world better watch out.

So in November of 2018 I launched my first course. I spent probably four months in the trenches, putting what I was currently doing on the back burner and learning a lot of new tactics and strategies, and I wanted confidence in myself that it was going to be successful. I had 12 000 teachers on my email list from blogging for those four years, and just collecting things for free resources. I had never pitched anything to these people. I had to kind of say, do you want to be a part of this? You know, because I'm kind of changing the way I do things. And I remember telling my husband, 'Okay, I would love to make $2000 but my big goal is $25 000', which would be monumental. That was my goal.

I 'opened cart' in November for seven days. And in seven days we made over six figures … it was life changing.

My first launch was $124 000. But here I was worrying that I spent $800 on Facebook ads. It was amazing. I don't know what it was. It was a God thing, had to be, but I did put in a lot of work.

You also spent four years nurturing your audience without really knowing what you were nurturing them for.

Yes, and one thing I have learned since then. I've done a lot of one-on-one coaching and I'd ask my students, where did you find me? That was always the first question I asked them in a call. And 90 per cent of them would say on YouTube. I started a YouTube channel and in 2015 — it's embarrassing, don't go back there.

And I just said, 'Hey, guys, there's this thing called Teachers Pay Teachers, and let me just tell you everything I'm doing'. So at that point, I was already flagging what my course was going to be about, but really I had no idea.

How did you decide on that first idea?

Most of it now is exactly the same content. We're revamping videos in 2021, but everything has remained the same. We've switched from a course-exclusive model to a membership model now, because we saw our students really needed that coaching component. So we have regular coaching calls. They have to pay for the course, but they also get this weekly coaching.

What's the price point of the course?

When I launched the first time it was $397. Now that course has transformed into a membership called 'The CEO Teacher School' for $49 a month.

I have two different offers now, our level one program called 'The CEO Teacher School' and our level two program called 'The CEO Teacher Academy'.

At what point did you have your 'I'm a success' moment?

Thirty minutes into that first launch. Oh, my gosh, I was crying. My husband brought me cookies. I called him and I was just a mess. He thought something was wrong. And because there was an integration with PayPal and Stripe I had it pulled up and it showed every second. The numbers were just turning; I don't think I'll ever forget that moment. I mean, in the first hour, I had made my entire year's teaching salary. What a feeling! I still can't talk about it too much or I'll start crying. I don't know how I got so lucky. The stars all aligned and it just worked out. And I was really worried I wouldn't ever be able to recreate the magic. That was a really big fear of mine.

How long until you did the next launch?

I launched in November, had the baby in January and launched again in February. At that point, no team members—zero—just me, myself and I.

So how did you even handle all the customer service? Like, I didn't get my login? And how do I get in there? And where's my password? And how do I find the library? How did you handle all that?

I didn't sleep very much and looking back it was probably not good on my mental health. But I'm a three on the Enneagram, so I wanted every email answered. I went live in the Facebook group every single day for probably an hour and just said here are the common questions in the inbox.

So, second launch, did you exceed the first?

Yeah, we did. We made $180 000 in that launch. At that point I needed to prove to myself that I could recreate the magic. So that's why I pushed to have that launch in February. I was itching to get it done.

Has it evolved in the past couple of years in terms of how you launch and how you manage that?

You know, 2019 was a very rough year. That sounds crazy. I had all of this amazing money coming in, but we were putting out as much money as was coming in. And for someone who doesn't come from money, that was really stressful. I wanted to hold on to it and never let it go. So there were a lot of sleepless nights, a lot of tears, plus I really needed to hire people to help me, so I just hired whoever I could grab first. I didn't have time to look for people that best fitted the position. Instead, my mindset was, who wants to help? I quickly realised, managing people became my downfall. I'm not a people manager. I work best on my own. That year will probably go down as the hardest year for me as a person. There were just so many failures, because students were vocal if something wasn't right, and I was the person who needed to fix it, and I didn't sleep until it was fixed. So I found out a lot about who I was as a person, and I've grown so much since then.

But 2020 will go down as the best year of my life. So I think it's just the ebb and flow. We both know James Wedmore. I got to speak with him one on one during that lull, when I was ready to let it crash and burn, it was so stressful. And he said, 'If you don't stop right here, you're going to lose this business in six months' time'. And he was so right. That day I decided to start fixing what I had tried to create and put the right people in the right places. And I educated myself as much as possible. Then I cleaned out the team and said, let's make it as lean as possible. Let's get this thing running like a well-oiled machine before we try to make it bigger than it is.

How many have you got in your team now?

For most of 2020, it's been me and one other person. We've just hired a few more employees and including our freelancers we have about 15 people now who help on a daily basis.

I have one full-time employee and everyone else is a freelancer or just comes in for a few hours a week.

How long did it take you to hit that $1 million mark?

About 17 months.

I've only had a launch go down (money wise) once, and we fixed it all. That was when I was in the lull in 2019, when I had so many people and I couldn't manage them all. And you know, in their defence, it was because of me. I take full responsibility for not guiding them appropriately. I wasn't in a good energy space, which I think had a lot to do with it actually.

Do you use Facebook advertising to fuel that growth or are you still sticking with the content marketing?

I do a lot of Facebook ads but we also do a lot of content marketing. And now it's a well-oiled machine that constantly produces new content. But we do run Facebook ads. I don't know what other people spend on ad budgets, but I don't think what we spend is absurd or crazy.

It's totally worth it. So I highly recommend, you know, putting in the money for Facebook ads if you have built those audiences.

The one thing I encourage my students to do, though, is to learn the things you're going to pay people to do for you, like Facebook ads, because then you can have an educated conversation, and get the results you want.

Between you and your one full-time staffer, you're working with a lot of customers. How many hours are you working yourself?

Now? I love my job. I probably come to work about 30-ish hours a week.

When COVID hit we bought a camper. I was in the office three weeks and out of the office for a week. I mean, 2020 was just so kind to us. So we were travelling and my family were all together. I know a lot of people had so many hardships and I feel for them too, but for me it was time with my family I'd always wanted, and we got to live this amazing life. My full-time employee works 39 hours a week. I'd put money on it that she works more than that, because she's amazing.

Have you got everything like systemised and automated?

I am obsessed with Amy Porterfield and Jenna Kutcher, as I think every human on the planet is. I've listened to every podcast they've ever put out. Stu McLaren, Jim Ford, James Wedmore—I love to listen to all of them.

One thing they all have in common is they work so little, especially Jenna. And it was mesmerising to me. I'm like, how? How do you make like eight figures and work so little? And it always came back to systems and processes. So in the past year I've read some really good books—*The E-Myth Revisited* was one of them—and I've started to put what I have learned into a system, but I think my employee probably deserves more credit than I do because she is very organised, colour coordinated. I just say it and she makes it happen.

What advice would you give to people who are starting out on their course creation journey?

I am a mind mapper. As school teachers we're taught to draw on boards and make things visually beautiful and clear. So I bought a huge Post-it poster and I encourage everyone to start this way, get all the colours and sticky notes you want and take every idea in your head for your course and write them down on sticky notes and put them up on that poster board, then stare at it for three weeks, a month, however long it takes for you to start saying, I think these things go together. I think I can clump these things together. That's how it all started for me. Then unit one went up on the wall. And I started grabbing those sticky notes and putting them there. That's how I fleshed out the course.

What the course is, its name and the transformation are important, but how you launch it is everything. You can have an amazing course idea that nobody knows about because you don't know how to properly connect with people. So connection marketing, to me, is far more important than what you sell. People will always buy from you if they love you and your story. But they won't always buy from you if they just love what you sell.

You come from a teaching background. Teachers are often humble strugglers doing a service for the community. How have you maintained that likability factor and lack of guilt around wealth?

That's the conversation James and I had, and when I was talking to him I was crying and it was really hard, because I did feel guilty for taking their money. I knew how much money they made, but I also knew we needed each other to succeed. So I was trying to be there for them as often as I could. And he made me realise I was running myself ragged and I needed to quit with the guilt.

I've just recently gotten past that point. Now I see that this program has changed so many lives. You know, some of my students are making $100000. One student made $45000 her first year, which is crazy. So now the guilt has gone, and I get to say, here is an example of someone who has taken what they've learned and put massive action behind it. It's allowed me to stay relatable to them, I think. I don't live an extravagant life. I don't ever want to live an extravagant life. I'm constantly trying to give back to the teaching community. I always try to ask them what they need and listen to them. We did lives throughout the entire quarantine that didn't ask for a dime. It was bringing teachers in and letting them share secrets that they had learned in teaching during quarantine. So when everyone else is selling we're trying to give. I think I learned that from Stu McLaren. That's been really important.

How do you deal with your new position and the extra exposure you're getting as a personal brand?

I used to be really guarded, especially with my kids and my family. I don't want to paint a picture like it's all rainbows and butterflies and sunshine. My students love me, my competitors don't. The people who were already creating resources don't love me because I'm bringing up the next generation, who will be their competition. So I get it, so my company can be in the conversations in those teacher Facebook groups. My students will screenshot them in an instant and send them to our inbox. We usually thank them for sending that but I've chosen not to read or even listen to those things. So that was a really hard pill for me to swallow, because everyone wants to be likable, you know? But at the end of the day, I've got my husband and my kids and if everything else fell away tomorrow, I'd still be the same person I am today.

How do you encourage teachers to step out of their fear and up to that next level?

It's a weekly process. I see them on Zoom calls, I know their names. And I point out their amazing qualities and particular traits. My team members do that as well. It's not overnight, it's day by day, little by little. Some of my students are over 50 or 60. They're just trying to make a little extra money so they can retire early. They don't know the world of social media and they're struggling in that area. Our job is to kind of embrace them and who they are and make sure they realise that what they're doing is for students and teachers, and that it's not about the likability factor. It's not for Instagram fame—the teacher Instagram world is crazy! We have famous teachers, like teachers with 200 000 followers. It's crazy. We can remove the vanity metrics and people just remember the why. They love showing up and we do competitions and giveaways. We don't force them, of course, but if there's a cash prize, if they get on and they show up, then often they'll get over that hurdle.

How do you build that community from scratch?

Getting to your first 1000 email subscribers is probably the hardest road to walk, right? I mean, those people are really your first true fans. But once you get to that mark, it's crazy. It just catches like wildfire, as long as you're feeding the flame. If you keep putting on the wood and doing the work, it's going to happen over time. The fire is going to get bigger.

When you say, I don't know if this is going to work, and you quit for a couple months, that's when it will die. *Consistency beats the competition, every single time.* I'm not the smartest, I'm not the brightest, but I am consistent. When I was building my list, I just tried to remember that I could chase all these shiny objects, or I could get really good at a few things. So I took what James did, and Amy did and Jenna did. I said, you know, these people, they're not doing a lot with list building. They didn't have 45 different opt-ins. They're not trying to bring people in for 1000 different reasons. They all have their thing, and that's where they're trying to bring people in. So instead of trying to be everything, just find the one thing you can be and then make it perfect. I'm still running the same opt-in I ran two years ago. So make it great to start and you don't have to keep reinventing the wheel.

What do you think you do consistently that makes the biggest return on effort?

I would say number one is blogging. We publish a blog once a week. Yeah. And I teach my students completely how to do that, because people still use Google, especially teachers when they're looking for resources for their students. So blogging has been very important for me in building that, you know, trust factor. But in addition to that, my podcast has allowed me to kind of rise to the top in my industry. Others have started, but doing a weekly podcast is a lot of work.

That's the best part of my job. Hands down, it's my favourite. And talking to people like you—it's so much fun!

Part III
Launch it out into the world

12

Build your digital learning website

Five years ago we built a website for my previous business on proprietary software for online tutoring class bookings. It cost over $50 000. When I had my first website built decades ago, I couldn't even make an editing change, I needed a coder for that. Now the technology is crazy beautiful and accessible to all. Like seriously, all! I've seen someone who didn't know how to turn on the computer build her own website in a month. Empowering AF.

When I entered the online course world in 2018 I tried four different platforms and found Kajabi a clear winner. Kajabi is an all-in-one software solution for your front-end website and back-end course hosting. I am absolutely in love with it. Good software saves so much time, money and effort, and it just keeps getting better and better. There are lots of options when building your website, so instead of my going through each of them, I suggest you fire up Google and compare them for yourself, and settle on the one you feel you could fall madly in love with. Okay, I accept that perhaps not everyone falls in love with software, but if it makes your life easier, makes a great user experience for your clients and makes you a lot of money, what's not to love?

In this chapter I want to help you put your branding to work and create your website. We'll be going over what content you need to include, how to write your sales page and landing pages, and, most importantly, how to optimise for student success.

As I've said, back in the day we mere mortals found it near impossible to create and maintain our own websites. Now you can build your own professional-looking website in a few hours. Sure, getting an experienced professional to do it is going to add an element of schmick, because they'll be able to do things that you can't, but do you need it? You want to launch and start making money and start having an impact on lives now. Rather than waiting around, bouncing design briefs back and forth, you could fire up your computer and geek out on the creation process.

What you need on your website

Figure 3 illustrates what your starter site map will look like.

Check out some other sites for inspiration, but start with where you are. In the arm of our business that creates online course websites for our clients, the most common request we get is, 'I want a website that looks like Amy Porterfield's'. Don't compare your start-up with someone's decade of work. It also depends on your budget. What I'm showing you in this book is how to start your online course business as quickly, easily and economically as possible so you can start serving your community, find personal fulfilment and make lots of money.

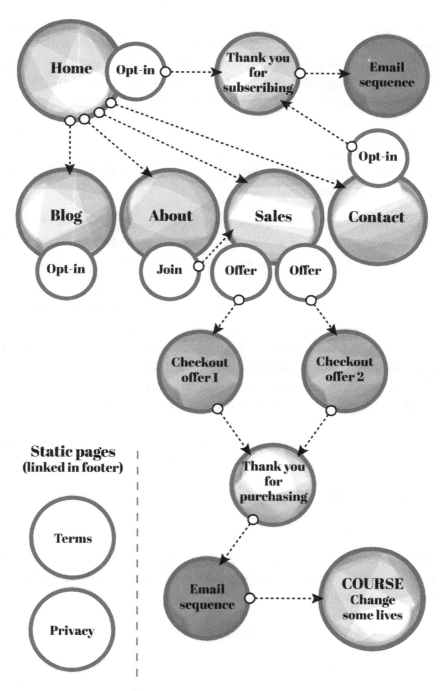

Figure 3: A Kajabi site map

Start small, but *start*. Once you get some runs on the board, you can begin to grow. You won't be able to build it to perfection then just set and forget. The journey never ends. You'll continue to learn and evolve and change along the way, so just get started and commit yourself to continuous improvement (what the Japanese call *kaizen*).

I can't tell you exactly what your website must include, as this will vary widely—depending, for example, on your subject, industry and goals—but I will introduce you to the skills that will help you determine what you need.

In the creative industries, a good website will likely be rich in imagery, colour and visual impact. Websites for an industry such as stock trading will be much more data driven and information heavy.

Simone runs a course that helps parents provide their children with healthy lunchboxes. She makes the meal plans and shopping lists all kinds of gorgeous. Her website is filled with popping imagery and a lot of engaging video, and it's really personal. Too much text on her pages and her busy parents would just click off. In the business world, though, a heap of text can work really well. Humans buy from humans, so inject your own personality into its pages. Use images and other visual elements that convey your message and support your brand. Choose pictures of you and your own images over too many stock images so your personality shines through.

These are your essential pages:

Home page

Your home page is the front door to your house. This is where people gain their first impression of you and your business. It will include the following elements:

- *Header.* This carries your logo and navigation menu.

- *Hero bar.* A really beautiful hero encompasses everything you want your brand to stand for. Think about your main message and how you might best convey what you're about.

- *Transformation promise*. Place it here so visitors will know straightaway who you are and what you stand for.

- *About you*. Briefly introduce yourself, then add a button that will connect to your 'About' page for further detail.

- *Social proof*. List any relevant (social) media engagements and podcasts, and add logos where appropriate. Any association with other trusted brands reflects on your brand and increases your credibility.

- *Your offer*. Entice visitors with your offer to persuade them to click through to your sales page.

- *Lead magnet*. Offer a valuable resource to your customers for free in exchange for their email and permission to start a conversation. I have more to say about your lead magnet in chapter 14.

About page

People often worry about their about page, imagining it's just a place where you boast about how great you are, but it's not. It's actually about your client. It encompasses who you are in relation to your experience and expertise *as they relate to your* client. It's about demonstrating to your client that you are best qualified to help them to achieve their goal.

When writing your bio (which I'll come back to later), don't tell your life story. Pick out the parts that speak to your credibility in relation to what you're doing and offering right now and your transformation promise. When potential clients read your about page they're asking themselves, 'Is this the right person to teach me what I want to know right now?'

When crafting your about page, think about what your client needs to know. What parts of your experience do you need to illuminate to convince them that they've come to the right place and that you'll be able to deliver on the promise you have given?

Blog page

We've already talked about the importance of consistently posting blog content. You can add that into your Kajabi site with a couple of clicks.

Sales landing page

Your sales landing page is going to be the biggest page on your website and is what will sell your course. You need to cover the following elements on your sales landing page:

- What are you promising those who engage with you (your transformation promise)?

- Who did you design your program for? Who is your target market/main customer?

- What qualifies you to deliver this?

- Why do you do what you do? What is your mission? Include a video here.

- What is your clients' biggest pain point/frustration? How will you fix this for them?

- Do you have a return/refund policy?

- Where has your expertise been featured? List media work, awards and podcasts, and include any social proof logos.

- Who are you (your short bio)?

- How can someone self-qualify? Include, using dot points, who the program is aiming at.

- What are three problems your client experiences and how can you solve them?

- What would it look like for a client who has a positive experience with the program and gets all the results they wanted? Paint a picture of what's possible.

- What's included in the course or membership?

- FAQs.

- Testimonials from graduates.

When you write your first sales page, write it from the heart. You can find lots of sales page templates, and may be tempted to copy the language used from pages you know have high conversion rates. But there's no reason to think the same language would work for you. You know your perfect client well, so put yourself in their shoes and write it for them. By addressing their concerns you remove their resistance, so it becomes a no-brainer to buy your course.

Don't overthink your first page, as the one thing I can guarantee you is that whatever you start with on your landing page, you will change it many times over the next 12 months. The key is to keep that curious experiment going and get it right for your audience, and take no notice what everyone else is doing.

Sometimes doing the opposite of what the rest of your industry is doing can actually work in your favour. If I look at a business course, for example, and it's got miles and miles of long copy, that really frustrates me because I just want to get on and do what I need to do. Some clients will already know you well from your content marketing, so when your course opens they'll want to jump onto your sales page and join without reading text for five minutes. Others will do thorough research before they enter their payment details. So start your sales page image rich and text low, then as the page scrolls down, allow your text to go into more detail. Include on this page several buttons to join your course, so as soon as someone has decided they're in, there's a button to click that takes them directly to your payment section. The purpose of your sales page is to make it easy for people to buy from you, so don't make it any harder than it needs to be.

Having one or two videos on your sales page will also increase the conversion rate, as it allows your clients to hear the details straight from you. Keep videos under 60 seconds where possible.

Welcome page

When someone clicks your 'Join' button and goes through the checkout to buy a product online, they're always going to be a little bit nervous about what happens after. People buy a course because they want a transformation. That involves change, and change is always scary. Your job on the welcome page is both to reassure them that they have made the right decision and to welcome them into your program.

The first thing they'll see at the top of the page is your welcome video. Woohoo! You explain to your customer what's going to happen from here and how to navigate around the site and find different parts of your program. This could be how to join the Facebook group, or what to do and who to contact if they get lost. This sort of 'housekeeping' is always located on your welcome page, which is sometimes referred to as the 'thank you page'.

Contact page

Your contact page is usually one of the shortest pages on your website. Being an online business, you may not really want people to be able to contact you. But no one will buy from you or stay with you if it's not easy to reach out to you. List the simplest ways for people to contact you—as a minimum, your customer service email address, your postal address and your phone number.

I use a generic customer service email address. This is one you can have your assistant look after so your day isn't constantly interrupted by fielding questions that are easy to answer. Most course creators will work from home (or nomadically from wherever in the world they happen to be), but you don't want to broadcast your home address to the world. Instead, set up a serviced post box.

As for your phone number, don't ever publish your cell phone number or you'll be plagued by calls at odd times 24/7. As yours is a global business, people will contact you round the clock so be sure to have boundaries in place from the start. There are many virtual office phone number services you can use. When a client calls, they answer the phone as if it's your business, and they'll take a message, which they'll then email to your customer service address so your assistant can get straight back to them. Each call will cost you around $2, and that's well worth it to you because it means that if someone has more questions they can ask them. But it also means your day isn't disrupted by fielding calls.

If you decide to use a closed Facebook group that's open to non-paying members, then add a link to this on your contact page so potential clients can join easily.

Lead magnet opt-in page

You'll commonly share this page on social media, so people who land directly on it have no other option but to sign up to your lead magnet. Remove the header on this page so there's nowhere to go other than to download or opt in to your wonderful free resource.

You can read more about the lead magnet itself in chapter 14.

Webinar registration page

Like the lead magnet page, this is going to be a brief, direct page that contains all the relevant details and makes the next step super obvious. Your webinar registration page needs:

- the title of the webinar

- the time of the webinar

- a clear opt-in registration box at the top of the page

- a picture and/or video of you

- three benefits that a client will enjoy from your webinar

- who the webinar is aimed at

- a timer counting down to the start of the webinar

- a brief about you section.

Terms & Conditions

The Terms & Conditions link will sit in the footer of all your pages, so it's easy for clients to find and check the terms of using your website and services. Check the legal requirements in your geographical area.

Privacy policy

The Privacy Policy link will also sit in the footer of all your pages. Check the legal requirements in your geographical area.

Next-level pages

If you have already built your personal brand and you're moving that online, you'll want to start with these added pages. Alternatively, add these after you launch your course and start working on building your personal brand.

Podcast page

We talk a bit more about podcasting when we get to content marketing (chapter 13). It's an online course creator's super content producer, so I strongly recommend you create your own podcast. Your podcast page lists all your podcast episodes. A player is embedded with a link to listen to your podcast on the most popular providers. You can create a separate page for each podcast episode, which takes a little more effort but offers a great return with SEO results.

Speaking page

One of the best ways to build your personal profile is through public speaking, whether on live stages or in virtual contexts. If you want to be invited as a speaker, create a speaker page or no one will know it's something you do. Your speaking page will include the following elements:

- your hero image, showing you in action

- your speaking topics

- the experience you provide

- video/show reel of you in action

- testimonials

- enquiry form.

Getting help to build your webpage

Kajabi is designed to help you build your own website. I love this because, as you've figured out by this stage, I'm all for starting your business without investing unnecessarily so you can get straight in and start making a profit. You will of course get a very different result if you hire a professional to build your website, and if you're time poor and cash rich or if tech is really not your friend, go for it.

But if you know your way around a computer at a basic level, then you can follow video tutorials and create your own. You can experiment on the page as you go so you can figure out what it is you want. If you want to build it yourself but don't know where to start, there are courses that will walk you through every step, or you can source some ready-made templates so all you need to do is change the branding and content. I've included some that I recommend in the resources on milliondollarmicrobusiness.com.

Here are some tips if you're hiring someone to create your website:

- Find someone with experience of the platform you're building on.

- Ask to see at least five examples of sites they've built, and make sure they align with your brand.

- Be prepared with examples of sites you like and don't like. The clearer you are in your communication, the easier it will be for your developer to deliver what you want.

- No one else can create your content, so be prepared to work with your developer to get it done.

- Your site is only as good as your branding assets. Don't supply dark and poor-quality photos for a bright and light website — it just won't work. Provide an abundance of great imagery that reflects the look and feel you want in your website and your logo.

Writing your bio

Your bio is going to be located in multiple different places, so put plenty of thought into it. You'll put the full version on your about and speaking pages, and an abbreviated version on your sales and home pages, then use a further abbreviated version in your social media profiles.

When you're submitting articles or press releases to other sites, you'll attach your bio there too. So you need to get it right. But in saying that, don't panic about it. People have told me, 'I've spent the past two weeks working on writing my bio'. That's a lot of time that would have been better spent elsewhere. Aim to have it done in no more than two hours.

You know yourself better than anyone does! If I asked you questions about yourself now, you would answer them right away. You wouldn't second guess every word, seeking some illusory perfection, before telling me. Your bio is a snapshot that people can read quickly to find out who you are, what you do and what your expertise is. It should establish your credibility and qualifications. It should answer the following questions:

- Who are you and why should they trust you?

- What are your relevant and interesting qualifications and experience? This is where you really reinforce why you're the person who can help bridge the gap from where they are to where they want to be.

- What awards, honours or media reports have you collected? Credibility and social proof go a long way.

- Who are you as a person? Try to convey a little of your personality so clients can get some sense of what you're about and into.

- What makes you understand this issue so well and why have you created this course? Share something of your motivation and what lights you up, because people will buy into that inspiration.

Answer these questions and then rework it into a 'story'. When you're a guest on a podcast, the podcast host will read this out when introducing you, so imagining it being spoken aloud can make it easier.

Optimising for student success

Don't just dump your knowledge into a course and think it will work. The best online learning depends on sharing an experience. The more of an experience your course is, the better you will perform over the long term.

I've spoken already about the terrible completion rates for online courses. I believe it often relates to the price point. If someone pays $10 to an online course marketplace, the chances of their following through are very slim, because they didn't place much value on it in the first place. If they've paid much more for the course, their chances of completing it are much higher, because they have invested in it more. When you've paid $1000 for a course you're going to want a return on that investment.

For the course creator, the key to success is enabling others to achieve. I don't accept that statistic of 5 per cent of people completing your online course. My pragmatic goal for my courses is a 90 per cent completion rate. My secret goal is for 100 per cent completion! I know it's unrealistic but I'm going for it because I want everyone to get a good return when they invest money in me.

I know the only way I can be successful is to make you successful too. Nothing would make me happier than if you messaged or emailed me after reading this book to tell me your course is launched and you're seeing purchasers coming in, and I get to share how wonderful that makes you feel.

One of the keys in creating an experience is deciding how often you'll stay in touch with students as they journey through your course, and where and how that will take place.

The easiest way to do it is within the members-only Facebook group or your community chatroom because it's leveraged. You can go in and address any questions and concerns and help people push through any blocks they've found. This will encourage progress, show you're invested in your students' success, and help them over the finish line. Often it's not the technical aspects that will block their progress, but unhelpful emotions and habitual behaviours. This is especially true if your course is changing people's lives.

Take this book, for example. If you follow the steps outlined, you have a pretty good shot at creating your first online course, which in a few years could grow into a seven-figure revenue stream and give you incredible freedom. The resistance you will have felt at different stages of this book will be what you have to overcome.

Earlier today I took a brief writing break when a friend dropped in for coffee. I asked her why she hasn't started ramping up her online presence yet, because she's amazing at what she does. Her response was, 'I don't want people to think I'm a wanker'. She's done loads of personal development and knows not to fall into this trap, but we're all human! So I know you're likely to come up against these emotional barriers. I'm tempted to invent a more articulate answer, but instead I'll tell you exactly what I said to her: 'Certain people are going to think you're a wanker no matter what, so you may as well smash it, help a tonne of people and laugh all the way to the bank'. Do you want to play small and watch while others are brave enough to show their vulnerabilities, put themselves out there and win? Don't watch on. Jump into the game and play to win.

Self-doubt will threaten to overwhelm you sometimes. You'll need help to push through, and you need to be present with people in your course to address their doubts. For those doing a course on changing a habit or learning something new, change is always difficult. And it's always scary. You need to have a process in place to be able to help people through that resistance.

I don't want to sound harsh, but you're never above communicating with people. I've done courses I've paid a lot of money for where the hosts have remained aloof and completely unavailable. In one case I paid $2500 a month for a mastermind at the lowest level, so I was very, very rarely personally communicated with. This really gave me the feeling that I wasn't important or valued. The leader of the program behaved like he was way too important and his time far too valuable to waste on personal communication, which sent a clear message to his members that they weren't worth much to him. I want your courses to be scalable and eventually this will limit your level of interaction with your clients, but there should always be a way to get a response from you or one of your team members, whatever the price point.

No matter how successful you are, keep personally connecting with people. Make sure you have a mechanism that's going to be sustainable as your business grows.

One of my favourite course creators is Brendon Burchard. He uses the Kajabi platform and is a great example of how to do courses ridiculously well. He's had hundreds of thousands of people through his courses, but somehow he has a way of connecting with everyone. As his business has grown he has found a way to make people feel seen and heard, which has been one of the main contributors to his success. It encourages people to want to complete the course successfully and leads to increased future sales.

Customer onboarding is really important. Think about that first touchpoint after someone first signs up and pays their money. Consider automating the following process:

- A welcome email is generated by Kajabi using their login information.

- They are redirected to the welcome page, where you show them around the program.

- They receive a personal welcome email from you.

- They are sent a printed welcome pack in the post.

- You welcome them to your Facebook group.

Ongoing communication touchpoints include:

- automated emails triggered at the end of certain lessons asking the customer to hit reply with their results

- milestones and recognition of progress within your Facebook group

- a plan for staying in touch, whether by email, text message or video call, depending on the price point of the program.

Action step

Get that gorgeous website built!

13

Content marketing

Content marketing will help you grow a business that is solid, strong and here to stay. I've used my Value Marketing Method to build multiple businesses (see figure 4, overleaf). It's the quickest and easiest way to grow a lucrative online company, which isn't to say it's quick or easy! It's all relative.

Some would argue that sinking a bucketload of money into social media advertising is easier and quicker, and initially it may be, but if you don't have great content marketing, and proof of your expertise and credibility, your success will be short-lived. What's more, it will soak up a huge amount of initial capital and continue to eat into your profits. Build your content first, then funnel advertising towards high-quality content.

The Value Marketing Method has eight elements:

1. social media

2. calls to action

3. search engine optimisation

4. third-party media

5. podcasting

6. live speaking

7. awards

8. publishing.

Developing all of these elements over the first two to three years will ensure your business is built on a solid foundation that will stand the test of time. Some elements are harder to rack up than others (think awards and publishing), but you can cover the first six from the outset.

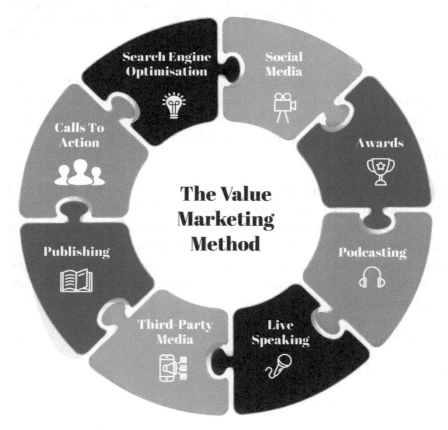

Figure 4:   The Value Marketing Method

It's so much easier to have a plan for your content marketing than to wing it from week to week and see how it goes. Without a plan, the task can seem overwhelming, which means either it doesn't get done or it lacks consistency. You create content so you can provide value to your potential clients and they can see what it's like to work with you. Content marketing is a means of building credibility in the marketplace. It brings you to the front of people's minds so when it's time for them to look for the thing you're offering, they think of you.

To create quality content, ask yourself, 'Why would they care and why would they share?' Create for your perfect client, and you'll find that your perfect client will want to consume it because it's relevant, interesting and entertaining to them.

Social media

As I hope I've made clear, if you want an online business, you have to learn to love social media. Otherwise you'll be making life much harder for yourself than it needs to be. Contrary to popular belief, social media is not about 'likes'. It's a wonderful place to create engagement, start conversations with your clients and build relationships. The social media space is changing constantly, so rather than trying to cover all platforms, pick the two where your clients hang out most, and learn to be really good at those. You should still create profiles to bookmark on all of the other platforms, but they'll be on the periphery.

As a course creator, your most valuable assets are time and energy, so you need to ensure that you invest your time to maximum effect. If you spread yourself too thin by trying to be all things to all people, you will be wasting both time and energy.

The most important social media platforms for most industries are Instagram, Facebook, YouTube, Twitter and LinkedIn. Other essential channels are direct messaging and live streaming. Let's run through them briefly here.

Instagram

Insta is my own favourite because it's so aesthetically pleasing. It's also the social channel that generates most of my business.

I'll admit to feeling a little silly when I started doing Instagram stories, but they are magical at brand building. With Instagram stories you can be more casual and conversational, sharing insights into who you are as a person as well as providing practical and inspirational content. The video element on Instagram has now gone into the next level of popularity with reels.

Facebook

Facebook is still the best place to drop links to your lead magnets, webinars and anything else you're sharing. The reach can be slightly less than on Instagram, but when you start utilising paid advertising, Facebook will become your friend.

Facebook group

For your own Facebook group, plan conversation to keep your community engaged and help them to accomplish the action steps required in your course. It's also the place to answer questions and run live sessions to connect with your clients.

Facebook group contributions

Never—I repeat, never—sell in someone else's Facebook group. It's bad manners. Be a helpful contributor and it will help your business grow organically. If someone asks a question you can answer, provide that assistance. Once you build those relationships, your profile will be clicked on and people will start engaging with you for business.

Direct messaging

Don't forget why you're on social media. You're there to connect with people, and it is so much more powerful when you can talk to them directly. If someone takes the time to message you, respond to that message or have a team member do it, so you can make the sales process simple and point them in the right direction. As you're building your business and you find you have more time on your hands, you'll notice when a potential client comments regularly on your posts. Send them a direct message saying hi and start a conversation. Take that relationship to the next level!

Live streaming

A live video will bring you a much better return on your time than an image or infographic. But yes, it's scarier too. To start with, commit to running a weekly live session in which you can get used to being on video and connecting with your clients. Don't worry if you're apprehensive in the beginning. You're building your brand from the bottom up, so not many people will show up at the start! You can make your mistakes in front of a small audience before you start growing. When I started building my online profile I ran a segment on a Friday afternoon called 'Cocktails and Coaching' where I would make a delicious cocktail and then answer people's business questions. I had so much fun doing this and attendance grew week by week. I'd then repurpose some material from these sessions for my podcast. From the main points I'd create a blog post, and I'd upload the video on YouTube. From that small segment I could create multiple pieces of content. It was a great way to generate quality content, make connections and build my tribe.

YouTube

YouTube acts like Google as a search engine. If you are in an industry where potential clients are searching for advice and instructions on YouTube, get yourself up on there and start your own YouTube channel. Sure, you won't have many views to begin with, but remember you're playing the long game, and all the content you create will contribute in the long run.

Twitter

Twitter is fast moving and content is generally a lot more short-lived than on other channels, but if that's where your audience is, learn how to optimise it.

LinkedIn

If you're in professional services, sharing your content and connecting with people on LinkedIn will be the way to go. Just keep in mind what is and isn't good etiquette. No one wants to be spammed with invites to buy your course if they don't know what it is and why they need it. Share valuable free content to build your brand and reputation, then ask for the sale.

Calls to action

Translate your marketing to business growth and convert to sales with call to action steps that are easily found. Don't go to all the effort of creating beautiful content for your audience and not ask them to take the next step. Selling is something you need to do no matter what business you're in. When you share your blog post, make sure to include the next step that clients should take with you at the bottom of the blog. When you're being interviewed on a podcast, share the link you want listeners to click on so you can capture their email address and continue the relationship. Make sure that everything you create and share spells out what you want clients to do next and that those next steps are frictionless and simple.

Search engine optimisation (SEO)

One of the greatest gifts of online business is your ability to compete with established brands quite quickly. You can be ranking high in search engines within a week of going live if you do some small adjustments for SEO.

Socials are optimised for SEO

Direct all your social media profiles through to the particular pages you want your clients to land on. When you're writing your social media bio, include the keywords your clients are searching for.

Use alt text on every image on your website

Alt text relates to the words you use to describe your image. They often won't be seen except in place of an image on a webpage that fails to load on a user's screen. The text also helps screen-reading tools to describe images to visually impaired readers. Most importantly, it helps search engines to understand what your website is about and to rank it higher in relevant searches. Take advantage of SEO by naming every image on your website.

URL names and page names

When naming the pages on your website, do so in a way that helps your ranking in search engines. Avoid dashes in your URL address and name your pages with what you do. Rather than naming my about page 'About', I name it 'About Tina Tower—Online Course Empire Builder'.

Articles with your keywords

When you're writing articles on your blog, include the keywords you know your audience is searching for. You know what these are by researching answerthepublic.com so you can write articles that include the most searched-for questions and topics around your course.

Wikipedia listing

Once you've got some content out into the world, create yourself a Wikipedia listing to build the credibility of your brand.

Google listing

Use a Google listing for your services too.

Third-party media

Even with the meteoric rise of social media, third-party media remains very much alive. Make a list of the media channels your clients are loving and create a plan for how you're going to get yourself in there. This could be television, radio, newspapers, magazines and all the media in between. Where your clients are is where you want to be.

Podcasting

Podcasting is such a wonderfully intimate medium. When people are viewing social media and video, they're usually on the move, open to multiple distractions and consuming only a few seconds or minutes before moving on. It's very difficult to hold people's attention for a decent amount of time on socials. Podcasts are a little different. They're often consumed while listeners are exercising or driving, and people will often turn you on and listen to what you have to say in full. People give you their valuable time and in return you give them valuable information that can help them in their life.

Every course creator should produce their own podcast. They'll be around for quite a while yet, and they're very cheap to start and to run, which makes them a great investment for the return they offer. You can set up a podcast and have it ready to go in a matter of hours. Check out the resources on milliondollarmicrobusiness.com.

To get some practice before you start your own podcast, become a guest on other people's podcasts. Find podcasts that share roughly the same audience as you but are non-competitive. Make sure to include a call to action so those listeners can connect with you easily. Whenever you're pitching to another podcaster to invite you on as a guest, think about why they should say yes to having you, so that you can communicate the value that you can provide to them and their listeners.

Live speaking

Speaking live to your clients increases the connection you have with them exponentially. You can feel their energy and they can feel yours, and you'll fast-track the relationship-building process. Live speaking isn't restricted to speaking on a traditional stage. It can be done in lots of ways.

Keynote speaking

This will be the format you're most familiar with. In a big beautiful conference room, the spotlight hits you, the music rises and you make your way to the stage like the rock star you are! Only a very small segment of the population find public speaking a natural skill; for most people it's learned. If it doesn't come naturally to you, now is the time to learn. You can start with small audiences and build up to bigger ones. Being able to present about your area of expertise will give you so much more opportunity to be in front of new audiences and to establish yourself as the go-to person in your industry.

Webinars — your own and other people's

Webinars were around long before the COVID pandemic, but they became a much more widely used tool in 2020, so now even clients who previously didn't know how to use Zoom can and do access them — because last year, for most people, it was the only option.

Once you've built a relationship on social media, you can invite people over to your webinar. Here's where you step up your content to the next level, providing seriously valuable content that helps your potential clients and then inviting them to join your course. Once you're practised, you can expect a conversion rate from your webinars of around 20 to 30 per cent, so it's a great skill to learn.

Alternatively, you can present on other people's webinars. As on podcasts, often other webinar creators are looking for guest presenters. This is a good way to get in front of a new audience and share what you know.

Conferences

You can run your own conferences or you can speak at other people's. Running a conference for your industry is a huge credibility builder and can be a life-changing experience for your guests.

Television

When you're starting out, the possibility of appearing on TV will most likely scare the pants off you and in any case seem like a pretty remote possibility. Don't dismiss the idea. Keep it in mind, because appearing on TV as a regular guest expert on a topic will supersize your credibility and trust levels. If you know someone who knows someone, which is how these things most often go, start chatting!

Radio

Does anyone really still listen to the radio? The answer is yes. Remember that the goal of content marketing is to communicate with your audience, expand your reach and build trust and credibility so your potential client knows you're the person to buy from. Even if they aren't listening to the radio, including the logo of a recognisable radio station in your social proof bundle on your website, bio and speaking kit will give you a boost. And it's super fun.

Panels

Participating in a panel is one of the easiest ways to be on stage. Keynote speaking was something that would leave me shaking under the massive lights as I stood in the centre of the stage with strangers just staring at me, waiting expectantly and hoping I'd wow them. You don't get that with a panel. There's comfort in sharing the stage with a few of your peers. There's the safety in numbers, but it's also a lot more casual, as you'll have someone asking you friendly questions to keep the conversation flowing. When your industry has a conference, put yourself forward as a panellist. If they don't have any spaces in the panel sessions, round up three or four people and create your own panel then pitch it to the organiser as a great value-add session for attendees.

Host/MC

The conference organiser already has the trust of their audience so when you host, that trust transfers to you. Hosting an event allows the audience to get to know you and get a feel for your style, and elevates your profile. The hardest part of all this is getting started and building the reputation to get invited or to pitch yourself when you have yet to gain any experience. Everyone starts somewhere, so just start small. Say a local person in your industry has just written a great book. Ask the local book store if they want to host a book reading evening at which you can act as MC and ask the author some questions.

There are many ways to build experience. You just need to go out and create your own opportunities. When you're beginning, no one is coming looking for you, so go get it.

Featured guest

In this wonderful world of online programs, people are always looking for guests to present on their programs to add value for their own customers. Being brought in as a featured guest automatically elevates your credibility as an expert and connects you with potential clients faster.

Sponsor

Sponsoring events in support of school sports teams or whatever cause you and your customers care about can give you a huge amount of visibility. It may also include an opportunity for you to speak or at least to sprinkle your branding everywhere your customers might see it.

Awards

Not too long ago I was told awards were a big waste of time. They might boost the recipient's ego but they did nothing to advance their business. Of course, this was from someone who hadn't won any awards.

Sure, not everyone cares about what awards you've won, but many prospective clients considering buying something from you online are trying to decide if you're the real deal or not. They're looking at you among others, and they're trying to figure out who can best deliver them their result. Being described as an award-winning course provider adds to your credibility and reputation. Winning awards also has a flow-on effect, as it opens the door to a lot more third-party media opportunities, speaking engagements and guest appearances on other programs.

It's not for your ego alone that you should pursue awards, though it still feels fabulous. It's always nice to receive recognition for your work and to have that public moment to thank your family, friends and team who helped you to get there. So start applying for awards and be ready to stand in front of the mirror and practise that Oscars acceptance speech!

There are countless awards out there, but here are some specific areas you can explore.

Industry awards

Nearly every industry has an awards program. People outside of your industry may have no idea it exists or any interest in it. That's totally okay, because we're only creating for the people who do care. If there's an industry award that your clients respect, you need to win that.

Local awards

These are easy to enter. Most local areas will have a town- or city-based awards program that awards local businesses across industries. This is a great starting point. Being a finalist or winner opens up opportunities for further coverage in the local media and in industry publications.

Perhaps surprisingly, local awards can sometimes be the hardest to win because so many people enter for them. No matter what, the experience will help you to refine your messaging and broadcast your business message to a wider audience.

National and global awards

Although going big can sometimes seem like you're shooting a little high, setting your sights on the major prizes can actually be easier. I have a confession to make: I've never won my local business awards, despite entering for eight years straight—I was a finalist every time. But I've won multiple national awards. The awards organiser at the local awards once told me they had 167 submissions for my category alone. One national award I won had just six entries. The competition was a lot smaller because most people will self-exclude. People think they're not good enough and not yet at that level, so they remove themselves from contention.

There's always less competition at the top, which is a great reason for becoming the best you can be as fast as you can. Many people are happy to embrace mediocrity; only a few are willing to go the extra mile to get to the top, yet it's actually easier than being average because it's less crowded up there. This is true not just of awards but of other areas of your business too. You're exceptional, so work on providing an exceptional product and experience, and embrace your place at the top of your industry. Someone has to be the best—why not you?

Then, of course, the logo you get to insert into all your marketing materials that shows you to be a winner or finalist of a major award gives a massive tick to your credibility.

Accreditation

As I've explained more than once, what holds too many people back from success is their own mindset. They feel they're not good enough, so they don't put themselves out there. There's always this underlying fear that they'll be discovered as a fraud, so they lay low.

We may know intellectually that we're good enough, but it's a natural fear that a lot of us carry, including myself if I don't keep alert to it. You started this journey because you have a yearning in your heart to spread what you know and to make a positive difference in the world. You definitely know enough and are good enough to do the thing you dream of. Sometimes you will be able to run an incredible course without the aid of formal qualifications. Sometimes they're essential. If you've discovered how to do amazing things on a skateboard and you're running a course on how to learn the tricks you have perfected, then that's all based on your experience. You don't need a diploma in skateboarding, it's your experience and skill that people are buying and learning from. To be a relationship coach, though, you'll need that piece of paper confirming that you know what you're talking about, before you start advising vulnerable people making big life decisions.

If your industry recognises accreditation, then get that certification so you have the credibility to do the thing you love to do.

Lists

There are lots of lists floating around the internet; some are amazing and credible and some don't mean much at all! When starting out you're in a race to build credibility, and getting on some prominent lists is a great way to that. Find what's relevant to your business and start submitting. Top 30 under 30? Go for it! Top 100 companies to watch? Yes!

Publishing

Publishing doesn't just mean books. That's the end of the rainbow, but it's also a lot of work and a big commitment. Start small and build up to it when publishing your work.

Articles and blogs on your site

You should be doing this every single week. As I've said, batching and repurposing will make everything so much easier and, most importantly, achievable. Don't be the best-kept secret in the world. I have seen too many gifted people with so much to share in the world failing to do the simple things to follow through on sharing their ideas. Putting your thought leadership out into the world can be scary because you'll feel like people are going to judge you. And it's true, people will absolutely judge you, but you'll learn not care. You'll reach out to the people who are interested in what you're sharing, and if you always come from a place of wanting to provide service, then you'll do just fine.

Second, people don't care about what you're doing anywhere near as much as you think they do. Feel that sharing an article every week may be overkill? Most of your customers, living their busy lives, won't even see it. Make a list of 50 ideas you can talk about and create them as you can.

Articles and blogs on others' sites

Sites need to be updating and adding valuable content constantly to stay on top of search engine rankings, so course providers and website hosts are always looking for valuable content. If there's an online site or magazine that your customers read, send them great content and ask if they'd like to add it to their site, with a link back to your site at the bottom.

Magazine columns

I hope print never dies! I am one of those people who loves to sit down with a good magazine or a book. To me, it's the most indulgent feeling in the world to curl up in a comfy chair and read. The quality of information you can find in a print magazine for an investment of a few dollars is phenomenal. You want to get your work in your customer's favourite magazine. You can pitch for an editorial so they do a story on you; even better for your credibility ranking is to become a contributor by writing a regular column. Find your customer's favourite magazine, work out what you could write that would add massive value to readers, pitch it to the magazine and start building that expertise.

Books

Writing a book is hard work. Believe me, I know! I love books. I love reading them and I love writing them, but it's probably the biggest mental challenge I've ever known. To focus on researching, building and writing a big-arse book manuscript takes massive discipline and all the mind games you can master. It is so worthwhile, though. If not for this book, you, dear reader, might not even know I exist.

Authoring a book is a respected means of conveying ideas and information. You are packaging some of your best IP in a format that can reach out to thousands of readers. If people love what you've put out there, they will engage with you and perhaps sign up for your courses.

$ $ $

In this chapter I have presented so many different ideas for content creation that it may seem overwhelming. After all, there are only 24 hours in a day. The way to turn your ideas into action is to develop an implementation plan and then have the discipline to follow it.

Planning allows you to batch your time. Focus on 90 days of content creation at a time. Plan and schedule your work to free yourself from feeling like there's an impossible heap of content to create and no time to do it. Keep a notes file on your phone or carry a notebook with a dedicated space for parking all the ideas you come up with. Then, when you're in content creation mode, you'll have a bank of material to draw on and can be super productive. If you're batching and repurposing content for different channels, you should be able to create 90 days of content in three days.

I've worked with enough course creators to know that if it's not planned, it doesn't happen. Weeks of procrastination turn into months, which turn into years. The time to start content marketing is now.

Action step

Create a content marketing plan covering what you'll use to get started on your first course.

14

Build your list

You have built your website, created your branding and set up all your social media content marketing. You know who you are, what you stand for, what you want to communicate and your pricing. If you've been implementing as you've progressed through this book, you've done a lot—in fact, you've worked your butt off. And I'm sure it hasn't been easy. There have likely been times when you've wanted to chuck in the towel. 'Oh my gosh, this is huge! She told me it was going to be simple.'

Creating a million dollar micro business *is* simple, but it's not easy. Many people will commit to getting started; fewer will commit to excellence and persist even when the going gets tough. But you can do hard things. You're not easily deterred. You know you want to have a go and leave a mark. You know that life can be hard no matter what you do, so you may as well choose a life that's rewarding both for you and for a bunch of people you work with along the way.

Everything you've done so far has led you to this next scary step. You're almost ready to launch, but the fear of failure is strong. As long as you don't launch, you can still cling to the belief that this is going to lead to all kinds of awesomeness. Once you hit go, you know it's the time of reckoning. You'll either sink or swim, and you put yourself at risk of confirming your deep-seated fear that you suck. Let me assure you, you definitely don't suck, and if your launch is not well received, then remember, it's all a curious experiment. Review pragmatically what you did, figure out what you missed, tweak it and go again. If you try and fail, give yourself a high five. Because most people won't even try.

Those who find success as course creators rarely look back on a dream rise when they aced everything from the word go. It takes time and experimentation to get your messaging right and create a great magnetic offer for your perfect client, to build a reputation by delivering a solution to their problems.

To get started, just focus on doing the next thing. Despite this book's title, and my promise to give you the tools to build a seven-figure income stream, that dream will seem purely conceptual to you until you have found your own unique path and proved to yourself that it works. Instead of being psyched out by trying to reach $1 million, start with more modest targets: reaching out to your first client, the first $1000 profit, then the next level, and the next. Your business practice will likely change at each new level. Reach your milestone, look at what you've done to get there, and decide what needs to change for you to achieve your next target.

When I finished my teaching degree I looked around at the teachers I admired and saw they were working ten times harder than the crappy ones. They were going above and beyond, changing children's lives, while other teachers just sat back and did the bare minimum to tick off curriculum requirements. Yet they were paid the same. I knew I would go the extra mile. Success is, after all, what happens when no one is watching. The thing I loved most about business was that I could turn a dream into reality right before my eyes, and as I performed better, I was paid more.

Having an employee mentality means you tend to sit back, waiting to be paid. If this is you, I suggest you set this book aside now and go and get yourself a job. But if you are willing to build it, push beyond your comfort zone and chase your dreams boldly, there's no limit to what you can create.

The day you launch, and every day thereafter, your success will depend on stepping up and proactively moving your business forward. I'm not saying that all you need to do is work harder and be super busy. You can stay busy all the time doing a whole lot of things that won't make any difference to your real progress. Focus instead on the things that move the needle on performance. Often they're the things that take you furthest outside your comfort zone. Bummer about that.

List building

You need to start creating a buzz before the event so when you launch you don't hear the deafening sound of crickets. While building your site, you have simultaneously started to build your list. As soon as the core of your site (home page and landing page) is up, you can start directing people to it while you continue to populate your course.

If this is an entirely new audience for you, you may have to start building your list from scratch. More likely you already have some contacts in the industry and a reputation you can build on. An impressive list isn't essential before the launch, as launching is itself a great way to build your list, but I'm all about making business easy, and the easiest way to launch is to have plenty of prospective clients ready and waiting to launch to.

As soon as you have created your lead magnet page in Kajabi, start sharing it in all your social groups and with your existing email contacts. If you have an offline, service-based business and you're moving it onto an online course, invite your existing clients to subscribe to your new business. Never subscribe people automatically—it's just bad manners.

The easiest way to build a list is to offer a really valuable opt-in—a lead magnet of some sort. I'm sure you'll have been there: you land on someone's website and they offer an option to download a free awesome thing and you're like, 'Hell yeah!' and without thinking about it you've entered your details and are smiling at your shiny new resource.

There are hundreds of different things you can use as a lead magnet. Here are a few ideas to get your creative juices going:

- PDF

    - checklist

    - guide

    - report

    - template

    - scripts or swipe copy

    - cheat sheet

    - resources

    - e-book

    - mindmap or infographic

    - planner or calendar

- video

    - resources

    - how-to instructional

- quiz

    - Interact or Typeform

- assessment

- template or template library

- free trial or demo

- discovery call

- webinar

- short course.

The best lead magnet is always going to be a resource your customers really want. Don't overcomplicate the process. Remember, it's simple, not easy. Ask yourself: What would provide your customers with massive value and what resource would leave them itching to take the next step you're covering in your course? There's your winner.

If you're doing a course on baby-proofing your home, a checklist of things to be aware of before you have a new baby will be perfect. If you're teaching people how to be home hairdressers, it might be a list of the equipment they'll need. One I've seen gaining great results is a quiz. It's a little harder to create than a PDF resource, but it converts quite well. You can share your quiz on social media so people can go take the test and see how they score.

The main thing to remember when list building is to be respectful. People get so many unsolicited emails these days; if they see you as spamming, you'll just end up with a tonne of unsubscribes. Don't give out information that's not valuable. As long as you're providing valuable content, your clients will look forward to receiving your emails.

When you're looking at what sort of lead magnet you can produce on your website, put yourself in your target market's shoes. Ask yourself what they're looking for already and what they'll find helpful. You need an appealing, catchy headline, but follow through with substance. People tell me they don't want to give something away for free, but this is a trust-building exercise. If you promise the world and they give you their details but find it was all smoke and mirrors, then they're certainly not going to take the relationship any further. On the flip side, if they go through and think, 'Wowsers, this is all kinds of fabulous!', they'll definitely be taking the next step. The more you show people what you know, the more value they know they'll find in your course.

Don't be afraid to share something awesome. Your email list is one of the most valuable gold mines you'll create. On social media people worry about likes and followers, but they don't mean shit without engagement. I see people on Instagram with 10 000 followers but no one is commenting on their posts, no one is taking action on their posts. It's better to have 100 than 1000 if those hundred people are devoted fans of your work and really engaged in your community. Think quality, not quantity, and do whatever you can to build that up.

Social media is vital for building your online digital business but it's not the be-all and end-all. We're at the whim of the social media companies, right? They could change their rules or direction and the whole list we've cultivated so carefully could disappear. Email addresses are safe. There's much higher value in an email list than in any social media because after an opt-in you've got people who are already more engaged, people you can communicate with more directly and more intimately.

Again, don't worry too much about numbers. No two list sizes are created equal. Work on constantly adding value and growing your list, but focus mainly on maintaining a high-quality and engaged list.

When I first launched my online course, I had a very tiny 120 people on my email list. I sold my course for $997 and had 11 people sign up, so I made $11 000 from that little list. I've worked with people with thousands on their list, but because they haven't communicated consistently or created it using values-based marketing, it's not responsive. If you run Facebook ads to build your list, your conversion rate is going to be much lower, because you've grown your list with people who aren't necessarily looking for what you're offering. You'll still get some great ones in there, though, so it's worthwhile, but size isn't everything.

Don't spend a year or two list building before you launch. You'll build your list by launching and you'll learn a lot in your first launch that will help you on the next one. You should be sharing your gifts and making money as soon as possible. Don't wait—do it. Accept that your first launch will most likely be small and that it's not going to be perfect, but you'll be fabulous. A small first launch is actually fantastic. It means you can communicate really effectively with those people and also get valuable feedback as you go. So go for it, build your list and collect as many email addresses as you can.

Freebies

Now, let's talk freebies. While a lead magnet is valuable and is free, I'm not a big fan of discounting or routinely giving away freebies. When you're starting, it can be very tempting to give stuff away to try to build your reputation and get some runs on the board. Don't be tempted to give too big a discount on your course or, even worse, let people go through for free. You are putting all of your most valuable knowledge into this course and you deserve to be financially rewarded for it right from the start.

As a step between a small lead magnet download and an invite to your course, look at offering a more advanced lead magnet, such as a three-part video series, a challenge or a masterclass. This works when you're not hiding that it's a sampler of your course. You're straight up saying that this leads into your course, that this small taster will help people decide if it's going to be the right course to solve their problem.

If, for example, you're offering a business coaching course for nail salon owners, it might be a great idea to do a very short course or masterclass on understanding your profit and loss statement. Don't give it such a boring title, though—something like 'How to get more money in your pocket at the end of each month' would be much more attractive! Once salon owners have completed that masterclass or video series, they'll see that you know what you're talking about. They've been given some valuable information. And they've come to realise how much they can improve their business if they implement the business systems you have lined up for them. They know they want more of what you've got, and this confidence leads them straight into signing up for the course.

The main thing now is to get up and get going, because while you're close to the finish line for setting up, you're actually close to the starting line for your launch. And I can't wait for you to start.

Action step

Choose the lead magnet that you'll use to build your list.

15

Sell your services from a virtual stage

Running a webinar and selling from that webinar will win you more clients than most other marketing activities you engage in. I've spoken about focusing your most precious resources, your time and your energy, on the things that will create the biggest impact, and selling from a virtual stage is definitely one of these.

Running a webinar

Running a one-off webinar or a series of webinars during your launch period is an absolutely fantastic way to speak directly with the people who are most interested in what you've got to say. Of course it's going to be nerve-racking if you've never run one before. We're always going to feel uncomfortable doing something in public we've never done before, but the only way to get over that is to just do it.

I helped Martha to build her online courses. Initially she didn't want to do webinars because she didn't like presenting. She told me she preferred to be behind the scenes and let the work just speak for itself. But humans buy from humans. When you're the expert, you need to get in front of people, talk to them, have a conversation. Once Martha started running webinars and connecting with her customers more personally before asking them to purchase, her sales shot up.

The perfect webinar is a pre-qualifier for your course. When you're choosing your webinar topic, pick something that people who need your course are looking for. It may be that you're pulling out a segment of your course. In a webinar you tell people the 'what' but you don't show them the 'how'. They need to be a paying member to access that.

When creating your website, add in a webinar registration page so you're ready to start collecting leads. For a full webinar checklist to cover off the technical aspects, head to milliondollarmicrobusiness.com.

Keep the landing page for the webinar as simple as possible, because a lot of the people who register for the webinar will come either off your email list or off Facebook or Instagram. If they're coming off Facebook or Instagram, they're going to be cold leads. They probably won't know very much about you or the course. If people are coming off social media, a lot of the time they won't actually show up for the webinar if that relationship hasn't been built along the way.

I run my webinars with Zoom because the capability is awesome and users' comfort levels are high. It's easy to run a webinar through Zoom, even if your tech skills are limited. The easiest way to get better is to practise. Before you run your real webinar, make sure you've had enough practice run-throughs that you feel nice and comfy with sharing screen, using the chat box and interacting with participants.

Once someone has registered for your webinar, do everything you can to increase the chances that they'll actually show up for the session. Because they aren't paying money to attend, people won't value it as highly; your attendance rate will sit around 20 to 50 per cent, depending on what you do in between. As soon as someone registers, take them through to a thank you page that includes a video of you that's under 60 seconds. Here's where you'll talk about how excited you are that they've taken this step, and reiterate the amazing things you'll be sharing on the webinar. You'll also send an automated email with the same details.

Plan your webinar content

Your webinar must be carefully planned and include the following elements.

Introduction

Introduce your topic, listing the key points you'll be sharing in the webinar.

Set expectations

Assure viewers they've come to the right place, that you'll be providing valuable information they can take away and use. Then at the end introduce them to the next steps if they'd like to go further with you. Conversion will increase when you're upfront about how the webinar will run. Surprising people with your offer won't work. People can stay for the valuable content then click off. Always be upfront and remind people throughout the webinar that you'll go deeper into this in your course, about which you'll provide details at the end. Keep it nice and casual, because if you're weird about it, other people will feel weird about it too. You need to avoid a clunky transition when you go from teaching to selling, and get comfortable with weaving the selling all the way through.

Set the parameters

The most common mistake in a webinar is overdelivering. This is a free sample, so don't wade through 50000 slides or maunder on for hours. Choose three points and:

- introduce the main idea

- address your audience's problems and frustrations

- show how your course will resolve them.

Invite participants to take the next step

You refer to your offer all the way through the webinar, so it's not being sprung on them. People are sophisticated enough now to know that if the webinar is free, they're going to be sold something, so there's no point in pretending otherwise. You're running the webinar so you can impart some valuable information and show participants what it's like to work with you, so you can remove any friction that might hold them back from taking the next step.

There's nothing more awkward than watching someone run a webinar who hates selling. They are in flow, doing everything really well, then they go all squirmy when asking for sales. Practise your sales pitch so the transition is seamless. Remember, it's the reason why people are participating in the webinar in the first place. They've come because they're looking for help. If you can solve their problem and persuade them that you'll save them a lot of time and money and heartache, then fantastic! You're helping people by introducing them to the simplest and easiest way to get their problem solved.

If you struggle with the sales process and the sales mindset, practise. Watch some videos, maybe even do a course on it. I recommend Colin Boyd, who is the leader on selling from the stage. His details are in the resources section.

Share the link to your offer

Sales are increased when you remove friction. This means removing any objection or barrier preventing people from signing up for your course. Include a slide that highlights the join web address. Have the URL ready so you can paste it straight into the chat box for your viewers to click on. That way they don't have to worry about typing it correctly—they can just click on it and get started while you're still speaking. When people start doing that, let me tell you, it's bloody exciting!

I'll paste the link in the chat box then let people know exactly what will happen when they click. I'll explain that they'll be sent a welcome email with their login information and can dive in straightaway. I'll let them know what time the welcome party is (if there is one) and when we'll be kicking off any live calls. The important thing is to be really clear on what the next steps are to make it real and take any uncertainty out of it.

Answer questions

People have given you their valuable time, so be sure to stick around and answer any questions they might have. This gives you a beautiful opportunity to show off your knowledge.

Once you've answered all their questions, say thank you and goodbye. The first time you do it the adrenaline will be coursing through you and you'll feel so proud!

Communicate consistently

One of the most important areas to get right when running a webinar is your communication.

Send confirmation and reminder emails before the webinar to increase attendance rates

Send an email to attendees as soon as they register, 72 hours before, 48 hours before, 24 hours before, 3 hours before and 15 minutes before (with the link to click to join).

Communicate with people during the session

Humans like to be seen. When you're running your webinar, ask questions and ask your attendees to use the chat box and give you feedback. When they do, acknowledge them by name straightaway so they know you see them. This will increase your connection, keep them in the webinar and help them feel more engaged.

Be honest and transparent

This obviously applies to absolutely every aspect of your communication. Don't exaggerate or embellish, just tell the truth and be *you*. Don't ever be someone else in order to get the result you want. You may see someone you admire run a webinar and think that's the style you need to adopt. If it's not your style, it won't work. You will only perform at your best when you're being authentically you. People will feel it, so embrace your own style and let your passion shine through.

Be prepared

The worst thing that can happen when you're running a big webinar is the internet drops out. One day I was running a webinar and I was at the 52-minute mark when there was a power outage and the internet dropped out completely, right when I was halfway through my sales pitch! I had my phone's hotspot turned on as backup, and 60 seconds later I was reconnected and everyone was still there! Phew. Always be prepared in case your main internet fails.

Check Zoom and be early

I once worked with a client who is a very successful businesswoman and had 500 people booked into a webinar. You *never* want to stuff up, even if only two people register for your webinar, but 500 adds an extra layer of urgency to getting it all done perfectly!

Five minutes before her webinar was due to start, she rang me and said her Zoom account wasn't working and she couldn't log on. I was way more panicked than she was. Letting people down is the stuff of nightmares for me. I knew there were hundreds of people clicking on her link to join the webinar from the automated email, and she wasn't there ready and waiting for them.

I couldn't troubleshoot over the phone to figure out what had gone wrong at her end so I created a new Zoom session on my account, sent out a new link to her clients and she jumped on my link to run the webinar. Not ideal, but luckily I was there with a solution. Afterwards we discovered that she had a trial of Zoom, which had expired, so her account was disabled. Make sure this doesn't happen to you, especially if you're new to this. Thirty minutes before your webinar is due to start, log on and test everything, and check that you're all set up and prepared to give a beautiful experience to your clients.

Check sound quality

In the equipment list I recommended a mic. I always use a mic when running a webinar to guarantee a better experience for listeners. It will also help that you can speak normally and not have to strain your voice or worry about background noise. Before your viewers jump onto your webinar, run a sound check so you know they'll hear you loud and clear.

Use Zoom webinar

I really love Zoom meetings because you can see everyone's faces. If you're on a public webinar, people get really weird if they know everyone can see their face. Especially if they log on expecting to be invisible, and suddenly their face pops up on the screen—eek! I once did this and caught someone who was in their pyjamas, and so embarrassed. Not the greatest way to start a relationship. So if you're running a public webinar, use the webinar function in Zoom and have attendees hidden and muted.

Remember to hit record

Once your webinar is finished, you'll email a recording to everyone who registers. Remember to hit record. So many people forget to do it. I know I have! It's understandable when you're concentrating on what you're going to say, especially if you're nervous. Stick a Post-it note on your computer screen as a reminder to hit that button once you've finished making small talk and are ready to start your presentation.

Make a waiting list

Creating a waiting list for your course is a great way to segment your database into cold leads, warm leads and super-hot leads.

When your course isn't yet open for launch it's a good idea to direct people to a landing page that will place them instead on the waiting list. This means you've got this segment of your database that didn't just go for the opt-in but joined the waitlist, so when you're getting ready for launch, you're able to market a bit more intensively to those people, taking extra time to reach out to them personally.

You can even do a special early-bird offer to your waitlist so they get a bonus and a bit of extra attention.

On your waitlist form, always ask a question that will tell you something about the person. Maybe you're offering a course on how to introduce the principles of feng shui in your home. You might ask something like, 'Why do you want to feng shui your home?', so when you reach out personally to them you can write something that's relevant to their needs. This is the advantage of being a start-up. You have the time to go that extra mile, reach out personally to prospective clients, and build your client base until your reputation precedes you and you no longer need to chase it so hard.

There's no shame in going the extra mile to win your customers. Don't sit back and wait for people to come to you. Put your foot on the accelerator so you can achieve your goals more quickly.

Action step

Create your webinar and set a date for the first trial run.

SUCCESS STORY

Tracy Harris
Mums With Hustle

Tracy Harris is the CEO of the Mums With Hustle online community and education platform for mums in business; the creator of the online Instagram course, Hashtag Hustle; and the founder of the online marketing academy, The Social Method Society. She is fiercely dedicated to supporting big-hearted women wanting to design their life first and their business second by harnessing the superpower of Instagram as part of a complete digital strategy. A strategy that aligns with who they are at their core and that sees them create their own version of success.

I chatted with Tracy in early 2021.

Why do you do what you do and serve who you serve?

I serve an audience of mums who are in business to feel deeply fulfilled by what they do, but who also want to contribute to their families and households and receive financial abundance, and who want to have the time, freedom and flexibility that so many mothers are looking for. So the women I serve are building businesses around their families and not the other way around. And I help my ladies grow and scale businesses by leveraging the full power of Instagram marketing as part of a complete digital strategy. I help them achieve their own version of success, whatever that looks like to them.

How did you get started in online business?

I was a primary school teacher on maternity leave. And like so many ambitious mothers out there, I didn't lose my brain entirely. I still had ideas. I still had a hunger to learn. I think once you're a teacher, you're always a teacher.

For about five years prior to that, I had been commuting to work as a teacher listening to business podcasts and online. I was listening to Brian Tracy. I was listening to Tony Robbins. I was listening to Pat Flynn. I started out one night, after we put our six-month-old to bed, brainstorming what I could do and sticking Post-it notes on my lounge room wall. When I say we, I mean my husband and I.

Because I was starting my own business, I didn't know what I'd sell. I was very brand new. So I thought I would share the journey because maybe there were other women that are growing at the same time, and they may enjoy the company. At that stage it was literally just only a community. I didn't have anything to sell, because I didn't know what my beautiful people wanted or needed.

I was about six months in when I hosted a meetup. It was for about 50 ladies from my community. The tickets sold like hotcakes. So first, I thought maybe I'd go down the route of events but I ultimately decided didn't want to play in in-person events. I was also 13 weeks pregnant with our second at that event so I was thinking about my life by design. I do like doing in-person events occasionally though, as there's nothing like meeting members in person.

Can you please take me back to your first ever launch?

It was called Hashtag Hustle. It took me six months to write and I did it very differently to how I would do things now. I'm all about the founding member launches and beta launches. I love that now, but I wasn't like that back then. I literally scripted the entire thing and recorded it direct to camera with a teleprompter. Oh, wow. I'm so proud of it and I think that's partly why it's still available today.

Also, I was 36 weeks pregnant! That's why I recorded when I had the opportunity. So anyone who's wanting to record a course and has all the excuses under the sun, 36 weeks pregnant, like a boss, it can be done.

Okay, so then you had both babies and went from Hashtag Hustle to where you are now with a membership and with a thriving community and with tens of thousands of followers and being the superstar that you are.

I'm going to receive that compliment. Okay, so then after that, I launched several ebooks. I also had one-on-one coaching, and I did about four, one-on-one coaching sessions a month. Because I was a mom, I didn't want to burn myself out and one-on-one coaching is also a really big energy exchange. Then we did the course and I was like, all of these things are working, they're all extremely profitable, but they're not that scalable.

If I truly want to reach as many women as I want to reach, still be super happy putting out the weekly podcast, and be this happy mama that can do all the mum things when her kids go to school, then I had to kind of look at the business model that I had. That's when I heard of Stu McLaren, it was 2017. I joined his free workshop series for Tribe, which is all about starting an online membership.

Because I was pregnant, I didn't launch my membership for almost a year after that. I just said, I'm going to take away the ebooks, the service, the coaching, even the course. And this is the only way to work with me. I was like, why pay $600 for one hour of one-on-one coaching, when you can join the membership and get group coaching for $49 a month? And people were like, okay, then.

When your clients have a course idea or even structure, what do you see holds them back from launching it out into the world?

The big thing that I see holding people back from launching their course or membership is this belief that everything has to be perfect. I mean the perfect course experience, the perfect sales page, the perfect email sequence, the perfect workbook, the perfect Facebook group for the company, the perfect social media graphics, the perfect webinar launch or challenge launch. People can move so far away from why they're creating this course and the impact that they can actually have on their audience and that can be their biggest block.

So I always say to my mentees, and this is something that I ask of myself as well: 'What would it look like if it was easy?' And that question allows me to tap more into my own intuition. Rather than leaning into that analytical side of my brain that has spent so much time learning from other digital marketers, and all the podcasts and the books, and everybody else's launches, it focuses me back on what's fun for me and how I best serve my audience.

I'm following the path of least resistance. Launching can be as complex or as simple as we make it. If we just work on getting the basics in place, then in our subsequent launches we can get a little bit more technical or a little bit more fancy, but we certainly don't have to start out that way. Quite often, when we are launching, we are launching to existing clients that have maybe worked with us in a one-on-one capacity, or who are now working with us in a one to many capacity through an online course, or who are our very warmest online audience. And so we don't have to fear not having everything perfect. The first launch of your course is often the most exciting and those first students, or those first buyers, will be the ones to help you actually improve that course structure and that course outline for future rounds. So go into it feeling excited. Ask yourself that question, 'What would it look like if it was easy?', and just know that it doesn't have to be perfect. The first version of your course is never the final version, but you've got to put it out there to be able to get to that point.

How do you recommend newbie course creators get started with list building?

If you look at your course as taking your students or your participants from where they are now to where they want to be, or the transformation that they will experience by the end of your course or program, and then just take one small little slice of that and create something really short and simple, that is going to give your audience a quick win.

This can be in the form of a simple PDF, or a checklist or a cheat sheet. Quite often we can be tempted to almost over deliver with our freebies and create free mini courses and free training that just take forever to put together and then just collect dust inside people's inboxes. I'm a big fan of creating a freebie that is really quick for the potential student to download and consume, but most importantly, to apply. Apply that tip or that process and actually get a result, and then let them know that this obviously goes way deeper inside your program.

I would also develop a key talk around that freebie or around the pain point that is addressed by the freebie, and then I would pitch myself to speak on various podcasts or inside of other people's free Facebook groups, or in paid communities as a guest expert around that topic. And then, of course, you can mention that you have a freebie where you speak more about this, and you can start building your list that way.

You've had huge success on Instagram as a content marketing strategy, what should the focus be when you're building a personal brand on Instagram?

When it comes to Instagram marketing strategy, you really need to focus on two things: connection and community. Because when you focus on those, you move from marketing as a means, to marketing as a way to start connecting with your audience through shared experiences, through conversations that unite not only your audience or your potential customer with yourself, but also unite the audience with each other. That's a really powerful way to create a movement that builds a sense of belonging, and a sense of family. Treat your Instagram marketing strategy as a connection.

Community is going to be huge in terms of driving your content and how you show up for your audience, but also your own mindset. When you think that you're showing up on Instagram to speak to real people, versus just looking at the lens in your camera, or posting selfies, all of a sudden, there's that fear of visibility. Or that fear of, you know, oh my gosh, I'm just talking to myself. Or, here I go again, posting another picture, who cares what I have to share? But with a community, all of those impostor thoughts tend to dissolve and you can instead step into actually serving and leading.

What does a million dollar business look like and mean to you?

I actually remember being really afraid of the idea of having a million dollar business. I believed that more money meant more hard work and less time with my family. And I suppose that came from societal conditioning, and also from seeing people in my own life who had regular jobs. Seeing how hard they had to work to get their six figure salary, or multiple six figure salaries, their jobs often involving being away from their family, working on weekends, those sort of things. So for me, I had this belief and I just couldn't imagine having a seven-figure business and also being present for my family.

But at the same time, having a million dollar business means I'm having a bigger impact with the work that I do. It also means that I'm able to do good things with the money that I make. I feel like it's a blessing and a privilege to be able to have access to the information and the knowledge and the resources to even be able to start an online business. And when you have that blessing, and when you have that privilege, you need to step up and make the most of that.

For me, it's a sign that my work is getting out there and having a bigger and wider impact. It also means that I'm able to be more present for my family and my children, and it makes me feel good in my decision to have my husband leave his corporate job. You know, for a long time, he was the breadwinner of our family and being able to even have that option where he could choose to walk away from that to be more present as a father and as a husband and just enjoy life and all of the hobbies and the adventures, was a really cool moment.

I don't want people, and women in particular, to be afraid of making this type of revenue in their business. It has also meant that I've been able to hire many women in my business journey, women that are contractors and part-time employees, and that is deeply rewarding. And, again, I'm just so grateful that we get to do that because we do provide a really lovely work environment. Our whole team is remote so they're able to work from home and at a time that suits them, and with their children around a lot of the time, for the ladies that have children.

What's the most exciting launch experience you've had?

The best, most exciting launch experience was for my first digital course, Hashtag Hustle. I launched before I ever learned anything about launches. So that meant I was just fully tapping into my own creativity, my own intuition, and just leading with my own heart, without yet having learned anything from any other external influences. I am a primary teacher, or an ex-primary teacher, turned digital CEO. So I just leaned hard into my knowledge and expertise as an educator and went with that.

The launch was a five-day Instagram challenge. I just opened cart on the final day. It was a Friday, we were at home. I didn't have a studio then, I just operated out of our spare bedroom where I had a little desk in one corner and a bed behind me.

I remember my husband came in, like we had a little cue for when he was supposed to come into the room, and he had party poppers, and he set those poppers off and he threw streamers everywhere. He brought out some champagne and we turned up the music, and I had a little dance. I just kind of said, 'Hashtag Hustle is now open for enrolment' and I was just so happy to share that with them.

After going through the five-day challenge with me, this really was the next best step for so many of them. And that was a $30 000 launch, just a bit over, and I couldn't believe it. That was my first launch ever and I just had so much fun.

Yes, there were likely many things I *could* have done, but it really was just me showing up in that Facebook group with the resources I had and serving and loving on these ladies. I was just so excited to get that first course out into the world.

It took me about six months to kind of prep and conceptualise that whole launch and course creation. I did it all with just my iPhone and a lot of typing with a very young baby in my arms. It can be done and it can also be a lot of fun. I have kept a lot of those elements in my future launches to always just tap into that excitement.

Part IV
Growth

16
The comparison trap

Once you start your growth journey, you'll find any number of shiny lights and distractions around you. You'll see someone doing one thing and think you need to go and do that, then you'll see someone doing something else and feel maybe you should be doing that too. You'll end up dashing in a dozen different directions at once and getting nowhere fast.

Have you ever felt dejected on seeing someone else experience the success you craved for yourself? Sure you have. If you say no, you're evidently superhuman. Social media offers so many good things, but one of its more damaging effects is how easy it has made it to compare our performance, our achievements, our life unfavourably with what we imagine others are enjoying, and to allow that to undermine our wellbeing. You see other people doing what you want to do, and you feel like you just don't measure up. This can lead to anxiety and overwhelm and block you from letting your own light shine. You see someone else's front-end view, but not the back-end view. You never know what goes on behind the scenes, what they're really feeling or what they've gone through to get to where they are. Social media is a curated and often distorted view of that person, never the full picture, and it can leave you feeling utterly inadequate.

I know it can be difficult, but I urge you to stay focused on who you are and your own strengths. Stay in your own lane. Don't try to be all things to all people; be you, in all of your glory, for the person who needs you.

Pay attention to how you feel about yourself when you're exposed to different people or content. Choose to spend your time with the people and ideas that make you feel good and help propel you forward. If you're following people on social media who leave you feeling negative instead of how you want to feel, unfollow them.

Focus on what you're good at, not what you're not. There will always be someone who has more than you and someone who has less than you. The only person you should be comparing yourself with is previous versions of you when measuring your own performance and progress. I'll use a personal example here.

At the time of writing, I'm 37 years old. I have a great marriage, two beautiful healthy children, a wonderful home, and work that I absolutely love and that makes a positive impact on the world. I used to feel like I was always falling short of my expectations. Using the sort of yardstick that a lot of people would measure themselves by, I've done pretty well so far. But the goals I set as a late teen and early twentysomething had me cast as the next female Tony Robbins! I was headed for absolute greatness, marked down to play big, and nothing short of that would be acceptable.

We don't always get what we wish for, and sometimes that's the most wonderful thing. After I sold my previous company and we travelled the world for a year, I thought a lot about who I am and what kind of life I want to lead, and I absolutely love where I am in life. I want to live a beautiful big life but am so happy with how much time I am lucky enough to spend with my family and friends and the multicoloured life I enjoy. I know there will be so much growth over the next couple of decades, but I'm no longer in any hurry to get there. I check in with my own expectations to ensure I'm better than I was the last time I looked and that the life I am living is my version of ideal.

I've made some terrible decisions in my life, but they've all taught me valuable lessons that help me make better ones. You have your own unique experience that shapes who you are as a human and what your priorities are going forward. Stay true to that. What's important for me may not be important or right for you. Don't lose your focus by looking over at what other people are doing. One of my life goals is to be invited to UN headquarters in New York to speak about women's entrepreneurship. It's a unique dream of mine and I make decisions in life based around getting closer to that dream. Once you figure out what your dream is, it's simple enough to make decisions that will inch you closer to realising it.

Social media offers us endless opportunities to fall into the comparison trap when it comes to the small things, like how many comments a competitor has on a social media post or how much they said the sales were at their last launch. But there are so many other things to take into account. If you believe someone has done better than you, ask yourself why and look at it pragmatically. Have they been going at it for longer than you? Have they been more consistent with their marketing? Do they show up more authentically for their audience? Have they gone all in? Do they have more time to devote to it than you? Are they investing more money in their education or advertising? Analysing the differences pragmatically in this way can take the sting out of the comparison and can help you make positive adjustments to your program. Remember, someone else's success is usually preceded by many failed attempts that we don't usually see. You need to train for the success you desire. Once you've trained for it, you'll be ready when it comes. You'll spot the opportunities that will deliver it.

If you have a list of expectations covering all the things you think you should be and do as a human, ask yourself where they came from. Make sure that what you're striving for is actually what you want. The world is full of people who work and work to realise a 'dream', only to discover it isn't actually what they wanted. Often we've absorbed the societal expectations we were raised on and can end up living a life that has little to do with our own deepest personal dreams. When you're living life in harmony with your own values and you truly embrace who you are, there's no need for comparison with others. You have beautiful clarity, certainty and calm in the way you live.

Use the example of others for inspiration and encouragement, not as a source of discouragement around what you wish you were or had. If someone is doing something well that you want to do, use it as motivation for healthy self-improvement. If it's possible for them, it's likely possible for you too. Believe that the universe is rigged in your favour, and abundance is here for you now.

Action step

Get out your phone and unfollow anyone on social media who is a source of negative energy.

17

Embrace automation and software

The technology now available to us as business owners enables the sort of exponential growth that some years ago just wasn't possible without a large team of people. I am all for doing more in less time and spending time on the things that we're best at and that create the biggest impact. Too often people run around like busy bees all day without ever achieving their desired results. One way to use our time better is to automate as much as possible in the business. With an online course business, there are so many resources available to do that, and more are being released all the time.

Here are some of the top software solutions and resources you can use to automate and delegate in your online course business:

Kajabi

Kajabi is the software package that will power the bulk of your digital course business. It has a full website builder that makes it easy for you to create and market your site. It houses all your pipeline marketing funnels, your checkout, your email marketing, your database, and your courses and membership. It's one of the most beautiful pieces of software I've ever seen and has absolutely changed my life, as it has for tens of thousands of other course providers who use it.

Kajabi is marketed as an all-in-one platform and it does cover most of your needs—but not quite all.

Stripe

Stripe processes all your payments. They take a credit card merchant fee and deposit the funds collected directly in your bank account. Stripe also sends a payment receipt to your customer. Single payments, multiple payment plans and ongoing membership subscriptions can all be automated through Stripe.

Google Workspace

Formerly G Suite, this package allows you to automate your custom email rules through Gmail. It provides you with Google Sites for your systems manual, Google Docs, Sheets and Drive for file storage, and you can automate your calendar bookings and availability through Google Calendar.

Monday.com

Monday.com runs the daily tasks in an online business. It's like sophisticated task boards. You can list all the tasks in your business and allocate them to different team members, write notes, mark due dates, set project milestones, track time per task and so many other things.

Not only is it good for day-to-day tasks, but it also tracks your launches and the many things that need to be done for a successful course launch. You can continue to duplicate and refine your processes for each launch cycle.

You can automate processes in Monday.com like onboarding new clients. When someone fills in a new member form, it can be added automatically to your member board with the client's address, making it easy to see who you need to send packs to. Loads of processes can be automated through this software as your business grows.

Canva

One year I spent over $20000 on graphic design, which was more than I paid myself that year. After that I did a graphic design course at the local community college so I could save money and time on creating social media posts, workbooks and any promotional material. At the time the only other option was technical graphic design programs—then along came Canva. Like Kajabi, it's a website builder for the uninitiated. Canva is graphic design software for people with no design experience. It's incredibly beautiful and will save you an absolute fortune and so much time!

The number of times a day that my EA and I pronounce our undying love for this beautiful creation is beyond ridiculous. What used to take a couple of hours to create can now be done in minutes. It allows you to have consistently brilliant branding across your whole business.

You can jump onto Creative Market and grab some templates to get you started, then watch a couple of tutorials, and you'll soon be feeling like a professional graphic designer. Warning: it's addictive! I could literally spend days creating more beautiful graphic assets than we would ever need.

Xero accounting software

Xero entered the market as accounting software for small business owners rather than accountants. As a business owner, you need to know your numbers across all areas of the business so you can stay solvent by knowing when to invest, when to pull back and how you're performing financially at any given moment.

When you process payments through Kajabi, you can have the whole transaction automated so it goes across into Xero, which records the sales so they are visible on your profit and loss sheet.

StreamYard

You don't need StreamYard in your business, but it certainly enhances video. StreamYard is used to live stream your videos into your Facebook group or page, or multiple locations at once. The advantage of using StreamYard rather than Facebook is the branding you can overlay on it. It means that when a customer is scrolling through their social media feed, yours will stand out and viewers will know exactly what you're talking about with your titles.

The other thing I love is the comment capability. It's difficult to really engage people on Facebook live when you can't see them. But when someone comments on your live video and you're streaming through StreamYard, you can click their comment, which will bring it up on the main screen. What a beautiful way to put your customer up in lights!

You can also bring in other people on video, share your screen and record the sessions so you can upload to IGTV, YouTube or your podcast for later.

Virtual office phone number

You really don't want to be in flow or presenting when an important call comes through. So I recommend having a virtual office to answer your calls. Being an online business, the number won't be called all that often, but it's a function you can easily delegate so you can maximise your time elsewhere.

Calendly

If you're taking any bookings in your business for discovery calls, coaching calls or interviews, say, Calendly is perfection. You can embed the calendar on your web page, specify what times you're available for appointments, and avoid going back and forth with clients trying to find an appropriate time. Calendly syncs with all major calendar providers, like Google and iCal, so if you book something else in the times you've specified as available, it automatically blocks your calendar. Such a time saver!

Adobe Audition

There are loads of software programs you can use to edit your podcast. Audition is easy to use to do the entire process. If you don't want to do it yourself, save time by getting someone on Fiverr to do it for you for around $30 an episode.

Libsyn

Libsyn is home for your podcast. Once you have your podcast episode edited and ready to go, upload it onto Libsyn with your description and cover, and it will push it out automatically to all of your chosen podcast listening destinations, such as Apple Podcasts, iHeartRadio, Spotify and Google.

Zoom

After the COVID-19 pandemic there aren't many people in the Western world who are unfamiliar with Zoom. In your online business you'll use Zoom for recording your screen-shared lesson videos, your meetings, coaching calls and webinars.

Otter

Rarely a day goes by that I don't use Otter.ai, which is one of the best transcription software programs. If I need to write a blog post, I usually do it with Otter. If I need to reply to a heap of emails, I say it into Otter because I can speak way faster than I can type. It's also great for providing a transcript of your podcast episode, which is not only helpful for people who prefer to read than listen, but also great for your SEO.

Later

I've spoken about batching being your bestie. Later is a social media scheduler, so when you sit down and plan out all of your content marketing in 30-day blocks, you can jump on and schedule all your posts and stories in one big hit, then not have to think about what to post until you next go into planning mode.

Dropbox

Dropbox is the easiest way to share and store your files. I keep mine in both Dropbox and Google Drive, because I have trust issues and dread the thought of losing my files! I find uploading from Dropbox to most software is quicker than uploading from Drive.

Quaderno

If you're based in a country, such as Australia or in the EU, that legally requires you to send a tax invoice to your customer, then Quaderno is a way to automate this. You can set different country tax codes and Quaderno does the rest for you.

$ $ $

There are of course many other useful software programs out there, and you may not need to use all of the ones I've listed. The key to software and automation is finding things you love that help you to perform in your business to your optimal level. If it gives you back time to spend on activities that can deliver you a better result, then automate that baby and go forth and conquer.

Action step

Head to milliondollarmicrobusiness.com, explore the software you might use in your business and activate your trials.

18

Become a systems nerd

Okay, I admit it, I'm an unabashed systems nerd. I find a thorough, easy-to-follow system such an incredibly sexy thing. Every time you plan to do something in your business, and you think there's a chance you'll do it again someday, make a system for it. I promise, your future self will thank you for it. My background, as you know, is in franchising, and when you run lots of locations and teams remote from each other, the only way you can get good at consistency is with gorgeous systems. I geek out on a good system because I know the brain space that can be freed up to enable you to work on the big things your brain really needs you to show up for.

Great systems allow you and your team to perform work faster and more accurately, and free up brain space to do what you do best — human creativity and delivery. You know the feeling when you're running around wondering what you're supposed to do next, worried you've missed something? Having good systems takes all that worry away.

If you've established the processes, all you have to do is follow the procedures that your kind past self set up for you.

There are many incredible software programs that enable you to document systems easily. Though I have my recommendations, I encourage you to spend an hour on YouTube looking at demos and comparing different options, because the most important thing is that it's software that you love and that makes your day easier, not harder.

I use Monday.com for ongoing, moving tasks and procedures—launches and business tasks that need to be done every week, for example. The reason I love Monday.com is not because of its capability. I mean, it's awesome, but so are many other programs. I love it because it's aesthetically pleasing and colour coordinated and when you mark an item as 'done' confetti bursts out on the screen. I am very incentivised by bursting confetti! Asana, a very similar program, has a unicorn that shoots across the screen. Ah, you've got to admire the human imagination.

I use Google Sites for my static systems and procedures—that is, the things that need to be recorded for reference but aren't regularly changed. This is where we keep things like our marketing contacts, colour hex codes, gift suppliers, admin details and so much more.

Here's a checklist of the information you'll need to systematise as you start your digital online business:

- admin details

  - company details

  - legal

  - phone and internet

  - car details

- finances

  - affiliate program

- – bank accounts

- – procedures for Stripe, Xero and Quaderno

- – insurance

- – accounting

- launching

- marketing

  - – gifts

  - – brand details and guidelines

  - – content upload processes for each social media program

  - – webinar procedure

  - – challenge procedure

  - – lead magnet development procedure

  - – asset creation

- new client onboarding

- member love

  - – gifts

  - – correspondence intervals

  - – exit procedure

- podcast

- regular (daily, weekly, monthly) tasks

- events

- team

- website

- goals tracker.

As I've noted, the whole purpose of creating systems is to make your life easier, so you need to document them in a way that is easy for your future self or team members to follow. Let's look at running a webinar as an example. The first time you do it there will be many little things you do—buttons to click and things to prepare—to get it running smoothly. Once you've run your first one you'll have learned some things that you'll want to do differently next time. So as you run your first webinar, record absolutely everything, from what to click on your Zoom setup, to how to sync with Kajabi, and right across to what you want to have within reach on your desk to keep yourself happy and comfortable.

If you don't record everything when you do it the first time, in a month or two when you go to do it again, you'll be racking your brain trying to remember how you did it or worried that you've missed a step. By creating a system at the start, you're saving yourself a massive amount of time and brain space, which will free up your mind to do what you need it to do—totally nail your fabulous webinar!

Whenever things feel really hard, I ask myself, 'What if it was easy?' Then I'll look at it again and think, 'Okay, this is really challenging me. What if it wasn't? If this was easy, what would I have to change?' Sometimes this shift in perspective will help take away that hard feeling. Perhaps I need to remove elements or tasks that don't matter and focus on what will make a tangible difference. Sometimes it means creating beautiful instructions so next time I do it, well, it's easy-peasy.

If you have a company of one, it can be tempting not to worry about creating systems and procedures. I hope I've persuaded you of the benefits of looking after the future you. If you learn to love systems for yourself, you'll get so excited when you start hiring your team. Set up a system defining exactly how you want something done, then when a team member starts, your guide will enable them to do an exceptional job. Everyone naturally wants to perform well. Often when team members don't work out, it's because the expectations weren't clear and the leader didn't set them up for success. Having a systems manual allows you to outsource and delegate and still get the quality you need.

Systems don't kill creativity; they free up your brain and thereby invite more inspiration. Clients will sometimes tell me, 'Urgh! Tina, I don't like all this structure. It stifles my creativity'. The exact opposite is true. I believe we can draw on a finite amount of decision-making and creative brain power each day. When we exceed this limit, our brain becomes fatigued and we're left feeling exhausted by day's end. You can maintain high performance throughout the day by saving your happiest brain functions for higher level thinking and creativity, rather than wasting it on tasks you don't even have to think about much but still have to get done. Then when you have segments of the day for creating content, serving clients and human interaction, you're ready to fire on all cylinders with your active refreshed brain.

As your business progresses, your systems and procedures list will grow, which is why you need to enlist clever software that's easy to use and easy to search.

Action step

Start creating your systems manual.

19

Your micro team

I chose this book's title because I want you to know what you can achieve with a small but mighty team. The only thing that defines your business as micro is the size of your team. Your ideas, your impact, your vision—that's all BIG. As Kayse Morris has shown us, with a small and dedicated team and good systems, and by leveraging the incredible technology that's now available to us, the sky's the limit.

I've said it before: the most valuable resources to you as a course creator are your time and your energy. You are the face and the engine of your business. No one else can do it for you, especially if you've built your business on your personal brand. So you need to keep yourself happy and healthy and to protect your energy, because if you can't perform at your best you won't be of service to anyone.

There will be things in your business that only you can do. As for the rest, eventually you'll need to find other people to take over or you'll burn out or limit your growth. My franchise business got too big for me to handle emotionally. With 35 different locations and 120 staff, the weight of responsibility weighed heavily on my shoulders. I knew that if I dropped the ball, I'd let down a lot of people who depended on me, so I took everything very personally and held myself to ridiculously high standards, which eventually led me to adrenal fatigue, burnout and the consumption of way too much gin.

In my current business I've been very successful, and have achieved that success very fast, by most standards. I know I have limited my growth by limiting my team and not delegating as much as I should have. I have feared building a large team because I love the footloose independence of going it alone. Still, there's only so far you can go on your own and if you truly want a scalable and, most importantly, sustainable business, then you need to learn to share the load and allow others to help you.

I am a recovering workaholic and control freak. Don't get me wrong, I have no doubt that my high expectations and ability to learn how to do all aspects of my business have added to my success, but what's the point of success if you're chained to your desk all day long and too exhausted to enjoy the fruits of your labour?

In my membership program Her Empire Builder, one of the exercises that my ladies do is a job matrix. Starting with a master list of every single task that needs to be done in an online business, they identify which parts of the business they want and need to do themselves and which they're prepared to delegate.

You begin by doing it all, because it's valuable to know what's happening and how it's all done, and also to save yourself some much-needed funds. Where possible, I would choose a profit-funded business over a debt-funded one. I urge you to make more money than you spend so your business is sustainable and you're running it from a place of abundance rather than stress and desperation. With some types of business, like those requiring expensive equipment, inventory or infrastructure, this isn't possible. But with an online course business, it totally is. When you're thinking of hiring someone to help you, ask yourself the following questions every time you complete a task:

- Is this what I'm best at?

- Does this bring me joy?

- Could someone else do this?

- What would it cost to hire someone to do this?

There will be some things that, yes, someone else could do, but they bring you joy so you hold on to them. Take client welcome gifts. When new students join my Mastermind program I handwrite their welcome card and put their gift box together. The client won't recognise my handwriting, and I could easily delegate this task to someone else, but for me it's important. This is the one tangible connection we have, and I like to put the love into that welcome card and pump that box full of good energy and positive juju from me to them. This is why I ask the question 'Does it bring me joy'. Because sometimes you need to stay in touch with elements of your business that remind you of why it is you do what you do.

If you're going into business, especially online business, you can't afford to say, 'I don't want to know how that part of the business operates. I'll just hire someone'. Depending on your level of tech love and exposure, you may not know how marketing funnels work, so you'll completely outsource it. And I definitely think you should outsource, but it's still your responsibility to understand how it all works so you can ensure the optimisation of all parts of your business then get others to implement those ideas. I see this often in both the tech side and the numbers side of businesses. You simply cannot be a successful business owner and say, 'I'm not good with numbers so I don't have anything to do with that part'. You may as well set up a little party at the sink and slowly feed five-dollar bills down the drain. It's your business. You get the benefits and it's up to you to steer your ship.

Now, rant over, let's flick back to who you'll need on your micro team for you to be able to turn your dreams into reality. Everyone needs support to perform at their best, but there are lots of ways to access support short of hiring a permanent team member.

Maybe you have no idea about social media marketing. First you can take a course on the subject so at least you'll know the questions to ask to set the parameters for a freelancer. If you're ready to accelerate your progress and you have funds to invest, get yourself a business coach to supercharge your road to success. If you have young children, maybe you need a nanny or an au pair to help while you get down to business.

The help you need to enable your business success doesn't always look like a traditional employee. One of the great time-wasters in my life used to be laundry. I always begrudged doing it. Now my kids are old enough to do their own and Mat does his own, but I was still wasting two hours a week doing just mine. So I enlisted the help of the local laundromat. They pick up the washing from my front step, wash it, dry it and fold it way more neatly than I ever could, then deliver it back to my front doorstep within 48 hours. Two hours of my life back, not to mention how much of a grumble bum I become when I'm doing something I feel is wasting my time, and all for the low price of $19! I can now spend that time working on things in my business that will make me thousands. Or I can use the time to have some fun and recharge my soul. Either way, it's a win.

When I was starting the online business, it was cheaper for me to hire a cleaner than a graphic designer but I couldn't yet afford both, so I got the cleaner and I learned some design skills for myself. You can do anything but not everything, so choose what's going to best leverage your time to help you achieve your goals.

Many advise outsourcing from the very beginning. Better advice might be to do what you can afford. If you're spending all your money on delegating to others but you aren't making the revenue to cover it, then it's completely pointless. It's a fine line between over-hiring and under-hiring, so I apply a formula. If your next goal is to outsource your copywriting, say, then work out what that would cost for 6 to 12 weeks, then when you hit that buffer, make the hire. As the business grows, keep doing that until you're doing only the things you love and only you can do. Do what you have to do until you can afford to do what you want to do. Having performance indicators to hit before making each hire will ensure you'll never run out of money to pay your team.

As your business grows you will progress from doing it all yourself to outsourcing one job at a time on sites like Fiverr, to hiring regular freelancers and subcontractors, and finally to building an in-house team. Freelancers and in-house staff are closer members of your team and can therefore impact the culture of your business quite dramatically, so always be very careful about who you select. Values alignment and attitude are often more important than skills for an in-house micro team member. Hire people who align with your vision, mission and core values.

Action steps

Make a list of all the job roles in your online business.

Highlight the roles you will delegate once you can afford to.

20
Outsourcing vs in-house team

Most seven-figure course creators I've spoken with have a team of between one and five people and use a combination of outsourcing (freelancers and contractors) and in-house or permanently hired satellite team members. Through my years of business coaching traditional businesses, I know that business owners often have one main pain point in common—staff.

Outsourcing means you have specialists on tap and can turn them on and off depending on the needs of the business. It's a great way of tapping into a worldwide network of professionals. I love to outsource for specific tasks—a graphic design job, say, or website updates or any project for which you can provide specific guidelines.

Because they're not part of your team and will often be working with multiple business owners at once, you need to keep your communication crystal clear to ensure a positive result when outsourcing. They also won't necessarily be a cultural fit or know very much about who you are and what your business stands for, so it's a very functional solution and you'll get exactly what you ask for.

You can use websites like Upwork and Fiverr to search for people who can fulfil your specific needs, or hire a virtual assistant. You can hire someone anywhere in the world who has the skills you need for the job.

Outsourcing do's and don'ts

Here are some tips for getting good results from virtual assistants and outsourced tasks:

Communicate clearly

Recognise that they're unlikely to be familiar with your business. They may have a different cultural background, and English may not be their first language, so clear communication is absolutely vital. Each task and project should be defined on your shared Monday.com board, along with milestone deadlines. Set out your expectations, and provide as much information as you can to give them the best chance of successfully delivering what you want. I have a five-page document about our brand, business values and mission, what we're all about and who we serve, so anyone we hire will know at a glance who they're working for.

Build rapport

Nice humans get better results. If you're good to work with, you will often get a better result because people will go above and beyond for you. In the agency side of my business that builds Kajabi websites, we have worked with clients who are rude and unclear on their goals and treat the web builder like a trained monkey. On the flip side, we have many beautiful clients who are kind and gracious and treat our web builders with respect. Who gets a better result? I tell you, when people are kind, there is no end to the extra miles we'll go to make them happy! Be considerate and gracious and people will do good work for you.

Have your systems built and available

If you provide systems to follow, then the job will be done to your exact expectations so much quicker and easier. If you have a negative experience on an outsourced task or project, check your process and system and work out what adjustments you need to make to eliminate friction in the future.

Share passwords via LastPass access

When people aren't a part of your core team, you need to take extra precautions around privacy, and only share the information you need to for them to complete the work. On Monday.com this can mean sharing a specific board rather than adding them as a guest on your whole account. In Google Sites you can share access to specific pages only. In your passwords, rather than giving your password, you can use a program such as LastPass, which holds your encrypted passwords and will allow the contractor into your specified account then revoke access when the work is done with a click of a button and without your needing to change your password.

Review and provide clear feedback

Never be too polite to get what you want. Continue to review tasks at set intervals to ensure that everyone is on the right track and you can make any changes before too much time is wasted. The clearer your feedback, the better your chances of getting what you want.

The in-house advantage

There will be a whole host of factors to consider when you make the leap from outsourcing to permanent staff, but when you do it's a game changer. Most online course creators start this type of business because it enables them to work when and where they want. If you're working nomadically or you don't want to bring a team with you, then you will either set up a network of freelancers or hire permanent staff who work from home. Project management software such as Monday.com is great for your in-house team, but it's super handy for keeping everyone on the same page when they're not next to you.

I love an in-house person who is invested in the business and acts as an extension of you. An assistant whose duties complement your own can project manage and look after all of the admin aspects of the business, allowing you to focus on creative or other roles. It all comes down to your personal preferences and how you like to work. Some people prefer to work independently, but I love to have my assistant next to me so that we can communicate clearly and collaborate closely. She knows me so well she can anticipate my needs, and she takes care of our clients so beautifully.

As soon as you can afford it, I recommend you hire a permanent assistant then slowly hand over the parts of your business that don't need to be managed by you so you can conserve your energy and continue building the business. Hiring a permanent team member is a large expense and a big responsibility (requiring a knowledge of employment laws, insurances, taxes and all matters relevant to being an employer), but it means you have someone to rely on and to help you grow.

Often people view staff primarily as an expense, but you need to look at what it costs you *not* to have a permanent team member. If you're overworked, you're not making optimal decisions and you'll definitely miss out on opportunities for growth.

When it comes to your team, gone are the old rules and expectations. Your permanent team member may have a desk right next to yours or they may not even be in the same country. The most important thing is that the system works for you. In my business, we have three office days and the rest are worked from home, so we can get together and enjoy that camaraderie, for example during strategic planning, but also have freedom and flexibility built in. I prefer to value work on outcomes, not hours. Once the expectations of the role and the outcomes are clearly set so team members know exactly what's required of them in order to do their job really well, I don't mind whether they choose to do it in or around normal business hours.

I find it easier to create a cohesive culture when I'm physically close to my team, which is why I choose to keep mine local. You need to find a balance that reflects and cultivates the culture you want in your business. If you're working remotely from one another, consider maybe sharing an after-lunch yoga session on Zoom and having regular check-ins and celebrations of good work.

The point of cultivating your team is to enable you to live the life you want while also scaling the business, serving more people and increasing profits. Create an environment in which your people can thrive so your clients thrive too.

Action step

Analyse what work arrangements would best suit you and establish a plan for when and how you will build your team.

21
Ditch the guilt

If you haven't been there, the thought of someone feeling guilty for being successful can make you feel like you've bought a ticket to crazy town. I want to talk about this because it's highly probable that at some stage this feeling will hold you back from achieving greater success, and when it happens it can be very confusing. If you don't recognise it when things start to flow easily, then rather than embracing your success you can sabotage it, because it seems too good to be true so you move back down to being over-busy and unproductive.

If you've battled through life, fought and tried hard for a long time, success can ironically make you feel uncomfortable. Working less feels strange. You have this niggling feeling that you're missing something.

This syndrome is especially prevalent in women. We feel pangs of guilt, like we're somehow cheating people if we make a good profit. We have centuries of social conditioning to thank for this messing with our minds. We're told things like, 'Don't get a big head', 'Don't think you're better than everyone else', 'Why do you feel you deserve all that money?' and 'Who's looking after the children when you're at work all the time?'

Traditionally women have done most of the unpaid work and unrecognised 'domestic' work. When Mat decided to become a stay-at-home dad while my business was taking off, people close to him would ask how he was still going to feel like a man when he wasn't providing for his family. Deeply ingrained societal expectations are hard to override.

Up until very recently, girls were raised to become good wives and mothers—and, if they were really ambitious, good employees. Not many were raised to become proud and successful entrepreneurial goddesses. Even now, girls are conditioned to be nice and selfless and of service to others. While I believe in the role of businesses as a service to others, they can only continue to exist when they're making a healthy profit.

Your bank doesn't discount your mortgage when you're 'nice' and when you discount yourself. In reality, the more money you earn, the more you can do in the world. Many of the world's great philanthropists are able to serve the greater good because of their great business success.

Psychologists define guilt as 'the perception of one's own wrongdoing or inaction'. You've been conditioned to work hard for every dollar, so that when the struggle becomes less onerous, even while your earnings continue to rise, it can feel wrong, even shameful. You've always understood that you have to hustle and struggle, and suddenly this core belief is being challenged. Once you find the formula for a successful online business through curious experimentation, you can be left feeling undeserving of your success, especially when you watch others struggle or when you yourself have spent years trying and falling short.

By giving our services away free or cheaply, and staying small, it can feel like we're part of the club. But pricing is perception. We charge more and people think we're worth more. There's a limit of course, but if we're discounting and undercharging at every turn, people won't value what we're creating. By doing so and keeping ourselves small, it feels like we're in the trenches together and part of the inevitable hustle. Blending in feels as comfy as a warm hug on a winter's night, so it takes a lot of courage to stand out from the pack. We value the feeling of belonging and fitting in, so when we experience and celebrate success, up comes that guilt.

This is why it's so important to surround yourself with people who are also having a good crack at life so as to normalise and celebrate your success both individually and collectively. Most of your friends and family won't understand why you want to do this. Most won't even understand what it is you actually do, and that's totally okay. Don't let it hold you back from taking risks and shooting into the stratosphere for the success that's waiting for you.

Most of the ordinary adult working population work around 40 hours a week, relax on weekends and aspire to earn a slightly above-average income. As an entrepreneur, your life is anything but ordinary. There is no clear separation between your work day and your real life — it's all intertwined, all part of this life you've dreamt up, so you can have the freedom to live life according to your own design.

Women are starting businesses at a much faster rate than men and leaning towards businesses that provide impact and personal freedom, which makes online course businesses a perfect solution. Guilt can be a healthy emotion when it brings to the surface something we've done that's incongruent with our values. It also can surface when it's time to reassess our values and beliefs and embrace the awesomeness within.

Achieving success, by raising the bar, may also trigger the fear that you now have further to fall. If you've experienced a significant failure in the past, this is definitely something you have to be aware of. Failing when no one is watching isn't too bad. You can pick yourself back up, dust yourself off and move on. Failing once you've reached a certain level of success, and there's an audience, can feel humiliating. It can feel like you've reached higher than you should and the only way left is down. This is where it's helpful to think about the people you look up to, people who inspire you. You may be the big fish in your local town, but you are playing so much smaller than people you admire in your industry, and you have so much further you can go. You'll find that most of the people who are much more successful than you don't waste a thought on feeling guilty for their good fortune.

The only opinion that truly matters is your own. Face up to your feelings and explore them. Analyse your ideas around success, and make sure they're your ideas and not someone else's. You don't have anything to prove to anyone other than yourself. Listen to your own inner voice and wisdom, and be brave enough to stand in your power.

You can suffer the shame of failure or wrestle with the guilt of success. Or you can choose a third option! Recognise your negative and limiting thoughts and keep them in check. Embrace the change and go forward and upward, feeling neither shame nor guilt, helping everyone you can along the way to forge ahead with you.

Success doesn't depend on luck, or simply working your arse off. It depends on making the decisions to do the things in your business that you know are going to produce the biggest results, even when they take you way out of your comfort zone. It depends on serving people brilliantly so they too can achieve amazing results. Success comes from creating opportunities and leveraging them. When you do that, you are worthy of your wins and deserve to have life flowing smoothly for you. If you're doing good in the world and doing the work you do for the right reasons, it can turn out to be easy.

Be confident and strong enough mentally to embrace your success. You have created what you set out to. You know that what you're doing is making a positive impact in the world and that you deserve to be beautifully financially rewarded for it.

Action step

Write down what your version of success entails.

SUCCESS STORY

Clint Salter
Dance Studio Owners Association

Clint Salter is an award-winning entrepreneur, business development strategist and best-selling author. He was just 16 when he launched his first dance studio business, and by age 28 he had founded and sold three companies and was named the Youngest Senior Celebrity Agent in Australia. Today he's the founder and CEO of the Dance Studio Owners Association (DSOA), the largest community of dance studio owners in the world. Clint has helped more than 34000 dance studio owners grow their business and have an impact on their local communities, and has improved the lives of over 800000 children through the programs and services he has created in DSOA.

We caught up in late November 2020.

Take me back to the beginning. When you started out, did you have the goal of building what you have now? Were you doing live workshops?

I had just finished *Jersey Boys* and had sold Dance Life, my previous business. I had some money saved, so I thought I'd take six months off.

And I got really bored, so I started coming up with different business ideas. I had a lot of single girlfriends, who were all incredible women, but they were struggling to find love. So I thought, I'm going to create a matchmaking agency dedicated to helping successful women find love. I didn't really want to do it myself, so I emailed the general manager of RSVP.com and sent her the idea. That didn't work out, but she said she found me really interesting and asked if I'd be interested in consulting. I started working there three days a week with the goal of rebuilding their live events and reversing the downward trend of in-person dates given the rise of online apps. Within three months I grew their events by 300 per cent, so they kept me for another six months. I introduced singles cooking classes and hiking and cruises and all these different events. And I thought, I really love this consulting gig. Around that time I attended a workshop with Matt Church from Thought Leaders, and he was talking a lot about intellectual property and packaging what you know. I thought to myself, 'Oh, well, I know stuff'. I'd run businesses, and I loved teaching and sharing my knowledge. So I just started packaging what I knew about the businesses I had grown and sold, and started working with small business owners to get new customers.

That was 2013 and 2014. One of those clients was a dance studio owner, then another signed up, and another, and I just kept getting dance studio owners coming to me, more than any other types of businesses. And that's when I knew I'd found my niche.

How did you do that at the beginning when you were so young? Did people take you seriously? Was your youth a barrier?

I had the dance studio, the dance competition, the online dance magazine. I then started a personal development blog with 20 writers on it: Make the World Move. That didn't last very long. I ended up selling that after about a year and then started the coaching and mentoring business. By then I was 27. I'd built and sold a couple of businesses, so I used that as my credibility piece. I was on the phone calling people. I wasn't doing the 'fill in my email form and I'm gonna send you 100 emails', I was doing outreach, creating lists of people, having appointments with them to sell them into one-on-one coaching. That was my business model—sell and deliver, sell and deliver.

Have you always run businesses with the idea of trying to create personal freedom? Because not many people would do what you had done and then say, you know what, I'm going to take a break, with lifestyle in their mind.

No, not at all. I would always make money and then spend it. I was still in my early twenties, I was in builder mode. We see it with so many entrepreneurs who just create and invest and keep investing and keep building new things. I had a real lack of focus with those first couple of businesses. I remember we had a very profitable year with Dance Life, our dance competition. I had an extra $60 000 sitting there and I thought, 'I'm going to create a boy band now'. I did this whole casting thing. I was going to be like the next Simon Cowell. So I created a band called Khoda. We flew people in from Melbourne to audition them. We got tracks done in a recording studio and had a photo shoot and a website built for this group. I was also running Dance Life, and this band was like my side project. But it fell apart. The boys are all doing extremely well now. One of them is an actor in Australia and the US. They went on to do great things, but just not together as a group. They lasted a couple of months, we got a contract to go on a cruise ship overseas and perform, but no one was available and it just didn't work out. But that was me. I was the kind of person who constantly created new ideas but didn't really stick with growing a core business.

Do you think that has helped you, because a lot of people have the ideas but don't then take the action to bring them to life, which you seem not to have a problem with? You get an idea and pull the trigger.

Back then I just loved creating, I identified with being a creator. I just wanted to build things. I wasn't as focused on the money side of it. I loved having money, but I never made stacks of cash in my early twenties through my businesses, because I kept reinvesting it in building these random ideas. I'm in a very different place now.

I didn't go to university. I went for four weeks and hated it, so I left. The first website I created for Dance Life cost $20 000. It was a directory, and I had to get a line of credit and three loans to build that website.

So you backed yourself a lot early.

That has been a blessing and a gift—the self-belief built along the way came from being a very different kind of kid, one who wasn't like any of the other kids in the playground. I had to back myself, but had just incredible support from my nan, and my mum, who always said, 'Just keep doing what brings you joy, keep doing what makes you happy. Don't worry about the bullying, don't worry about what other people say. You're incredible and just keep doing the things you love'.

I'm extremely lucky. I was going to the bank at 21 and getting these loans and she couldn't be the guarantor because she wasn't making enough money to cover any of the loans. So I had to go to different banks to get $3000 here, $5000 there, and she would just say, 'Yeah, go for it!'

How was the fear of failure for you at that age? Were you worried that you wouldn't be able to pay those loans back?

I've never really been afraid of failing. I think the meaning of failing can depend on how you've grown up and what failure has meant in your family. I could say that I failed with parts of my dance studio, the boy band and the matchmaking agency—they could all be seen as failures. But I've never actually looked at any of those things like that. No matter what gets thrown at me, I know I'll be able to make it through. I think that way of thinking has also protected me a bit whenever I think something won't work. I just say to myself, 'If it doesn't work, it doesn't matter'.

How long did it take you to make the jump from where you were drawing in a few dance studio owners to going, 'You know what, I'm going to cut off everything else, double down and become the dance studio guy'?

It was the scariest decision. It was the end of 2014. I'd been doing one-on-one coaching for about 18 months and I was getting so frustrated.

I kept answering the same questions all the time. I literally could record myself and just press play on every coaching call. I knew there had to be a better way. I was working six days a week, eight hours a day coaching at that point. I was exhausted and started getting annoyed with people.

I started looking online for ideas, and I came across Brendon Burchard and one of his online programs, Total Product Blueprint. I learned how to package up your IP in a really leveraged way, in a way that could scale, in a way that didn't involve me sitting one-on-one with someone. So I thought, 'I'm going to build an online program for dance studios'. At the beginning I thought that would serve the dance market and I would just keep doing my one-on-one coaching outside of dance. That was my goal. I launched it online for the studios in August 2014, and I made $5000 in a 90-minute webinar. I remember calling my mum crying. That was it, I just did it. I thought the webinar was good, so I ran a webinar every week live. At the same time, I'm still doing all my coaching. Then I had dinner with a friend and she said, 'Maybe you should just be the dance guy'. I was afraid because I thought, 'Are there enough studios?' That was my first concern, and 'Do they have enough money?' was my second question. 'Are there enough of them for this to sustain me as an income? And do they have enough money to be able to pay me for what I'm sharing?' That was the challenge. I ended up tricking myself into trying it by framing it in my mind as an experiment, so after a year I could go back to what I'd been doing if it didn't work out.

That's how I do everything now in our business. Everything is an experiment. It also allows you not to create too much attachment to the idea. Even though I had a laid-back approach to ideas, there was still a level of 'this has to work'. I would get over it really quickly if it didn't work out, but I still had an attachment. So now everything's just an experiment. Let's try it. Let's see how it goes. Draw a line in the sand, give it a date. That's what I do when working with studio owners. And then my focus was on going deep, deep, deep in serving them, you know, unconditionally, to help them with their challenges.

I didn't think it would look like this. My wish was, 'I want to make a million dollars. And I want one team member'. That was my goal. I wanted a million dollars and one staff member because, for me, team had always meant pain. More people, more pain. So the vision in my head was a million dollar business, a virtual assistant—I'm good to go.

How long did it take you to get to that?

In 2017 we did just over a million dollars.

How many team members did you have then?

We had two, but I was working harder than I've ever worked in my life. I did the Facebook ads, wrote the copy, did all the programming. I still did some customer service, I did all the coaching. We had no coaches, no experts—it was the Clint Show. Being in mastermind groups and working with different people, I kept hearing people talk about the team and the art of delegation that gives you freedom. So that's when I thought, okay, I might need to get serious about bringing in the right types of people to help us continue to build the vision I had for the business.

If you had delegated earlier, and it hadn't been the Clint Show, do you think you would have been able to get it to the million and reach that critical mass?

No, it needed to be driven by me. And the secret is, it still has to be driven by me. And as much as I don't want the Dance Studio Owners Association to be about Clint, it's still about Clint. We've done a great job bringing in our coaches, and I take a few calls a month. We've done a great job of getting me out of it and bringing in incredible experts and sharing the knowledge of others. But people buy from people, and at the end of the day I'm running the free training, I'm creating the content, I'm the person they're coming to the business for.

What shift did you make to get that freedom back and stop working all day?

I think a lot of people have that million dollar goal, and at first it's a really great milestone, but when I hit it I was like, well now what do I do? I don't really need any more money, a million dollars a year is great, so it had to be about something bigger than the dollars. It had to be about me loving my work.

At that point, I was doing so many things. I'd gotten away from doing what I love because I had to run the business. The next goal for me was: 'How can I create a role for myself that just fills me up and gives me a lot of joy? What would I be doing all day if I wasn't cracking the whip over my team members? So I made that list, I did a time audit, I got really clear on where I was spending my time and where I wanted to spend more of it, and then hired for those gaps.

For example, I don't want to run our projects anymore. Okay, let's bring on a project manager. And that was like one of the first core roles we brought on part time—they were just part time. Then we had a marketing jack-of-all-trades person who could do a bit of everything—a bit of copy, a bit of funnels, a bit of website building. Then we got the person who could specifically do ads, then we started bringing on coaches so I could free up my time a little more. I could give our members different insights and perspectives, which was really important.

Then you stop and realise: when you give yourself the time to focus on the things you love, as the CEO grows the business, the business gets better, bigger, right? It grows, and you get to impact more people. You welcome more customers, more clients, more members, and the thing doesn't fall apart, because you've got team members who are creating systems, following systems and executing on the day-to-day operations of the business.

Do you know how many hours you would work now?

I'm always doing something. I'm always doing stuff, but actual, mandatory work? I go to our team meeting and then I work about 16 hours a week. Which means I get a lot of time to work on improving our membership levels to ensure we provide the best training in the industry. I had one call today, and now I'm working on one of our memberships and reimagining that for next year, so I get to spend like four hours on that.

So you're at the helicopter level?

Yes, definitely the helicopter level. The game changer was when the Operations Director started full-time two years ago, which was a real blessing.

I'm okay with not doing the day-to-day stuff. The team need me to focus on the big picture so we can keep growing the business and impacting the lives of tens of thousands of people, so we can keep growing and paying team members more money and enabling them to have a great life with their family. We have a lot of flexibility. We have no set working hours. They simply have to deliver on their roles. My philosophy is, if you don't do your job, I'm gonna care, but if you do your job, you can work at 2 am if you want, I don't mind. So there's a lot of flexibility for them, because that's how I work too.

Did you ever feel guilty when you started making a lot of money?

I don't think so. I've never felt like that because I've worked hard and I'm proud of the work I've done. Making money is just one type of currency. I've been able to make money and now I can make a difference. We helped build a school in Kenya, I just sent money to my mum and she got a new roof on her apartment, I've moved in with my partner's parents so we can look after them. Money is an incredible vehicle to do great things in the world. So I've never been uncomfortable about making a lot of it, because I truly feel like I deserve it.

Since the business has grown up, have you had another moment like the one you described at that webinar when you made $5000?

Yes, just last week I was able to give our team two months' salary as a bonus. I got off that call and cried for five minutes. I so appreciated what they'd contributed to our business over the past 12 months, and the impact that has made on our thousands of members. We've changed so many lives this year, and in that moment that thought made me highly emotional. I've cried a lot this year, not out of sadness but just out of appreciation. You know, I ran a two-day planning intensive for our members where we mapped out a year together, and for the last five minutes I was a mess. I was just telling them how proud I was of them. So the important moments aren't about more money, they're about people's lives, and being part of that transformation is very powerful.

How do you manage the growth when you've grown so rapidly?

The crazy thing is that as we keep growing, our profit grows. First you've got to focus on the dollars coming in and going out, and you've got to know what's bringing in revenue and what's making you profit. Some people have different revenue streams in their business, and they're putting time and energy into some that are losing money. It doesn't make any sense.

Over these last six years at DSOA, I print out the P&L report every month. I get the red pen out and go through it fanatically looking for anything going out that shouldn't, anything I need to flag. We've got bookkeepers, accountants, our operations director is an ex-CFO, but I'm still on top of it. If those birthday flowers go out, and they're $54, I say, 'Guys, our budget is $50', and they say, 'But it's just $4!' And I say, 'Yes, but we have over 200 members, so $4 times 200—that's your bonus'. People tend to be good with money at the beginning, then they go through this stage when they see more than they ever have coming in, and they spend it.

Just because you have it doesn't mean you should spend it. I focus on profitability. We've killed things off in our business that have been profitable, but have taken away time and energy and resources from the team that could be better spent in another revenue stream that's doing better. We used to sell everything and now we really sell two things.

You've got to know what your team is working on and ensure they are being productive and efficient and effective with their time. My team fill timesheets every day. I know what my team do every 15 minutes. People say, 'But that means you don't trust them'. No, I trust them. But we feed that data into our P&L. If someone's spending 15 hours on a revenue stream, I want those 15 hours of their wage to go into my P&L, so I get true profitability. I'm not just seeing someone's salary split across two things evenly; they might have spent 80 per cent of their time in one area and 20 per cent in the other. So we're always looking at that data to check. Every quarter, we're reviewing those reports, and we're making changes to our business because of it.

How many people have you got in your team now?

We have two full-time team members. Then we have five in the core team who are contractors working anywhere from 10 to 20 hours a week.

And that's with the business doing multiple millions a year?

Yes.

I've got friends who are creating the same or less revenue, and have much bigger teams. Getting the right people on board, working with them, mentoring them, managing them and ensuring they're being effective with their time is important. I have no worries getting rid of people. It's efficiency, quality work and culture fit I'm focused on.

How do you keep connected when they're working from home?

You know what, everyone loves their life outside of DSOA. We always joke because one of our guys lives in a new country every month. The other one is always at the beach. We employ lots of mums as well, so they're with their kids and they're doing the school pick-up, and we've got some young people who just like travelling and hanging out with their friends. So DSOA is not their life. I'm cool with that—it doesn't need to be your life. You just need to get the work done when you're here. I think working your own hours, from wherever you want, and getting paid to produce great work, means they get to have so much joy outside of their work and it shows in what they do for us. They're not miserable. They love life. They love their job. The result of that is that we get more out of our team because they are happy both at work and outside of work.

So, location freedom. You left for New York City at about the time you hit that seven figures, right?

Yes, and I remember thinking, 'Wow, New York rent is expensive. I've made a million dollars, now I can spend it on rent'. I was always a bit of a gypsy, in Australia and in Sydney. I like to move a lot and to live in different apartments. But I just love New York. I'd been visiting New York every year for about seven years to go to the Broadway shows. The city felt like home to me. When I got a visa to work in the US, I had dinner with an American friend who was visiting Australia at the time, and she said, 'Every time I see you in New York, you're like a different person. You're so happy, so relaxed. I feel like that's where you need to be'. That night I went home and emailed a broker in New York and said, 'I'm going to move to New York in eight weeks. Find me an apartment', and that was it. I woke up the next morning after the bottle of wine and thought that probably wasn't the best idea, but then, you know what, I've got nothing to lose, and I'll regret it if I don't go now. I've got the visa. Let's do this.

What are the benefits of living and working from anywhere?

Seventy per cent of our customers are in the US, so not having to stay awake until midnight or wake up at 3 am is really helpful. But, other than that, and the couple of live events we host in the US each year, our business runs entirely online. We could live anywhere, and our team could live and work from anywhere.

I think these types of businesses are important and impactful and can change not only your life but many lives, you know—your team, your customers, their families, their customers. It's a beautiful snowball effect, the impact of sharing your message, your wisdom and your insight with others over the internet, beamed across the globe. It's incredible.

So you're still designing life your way, as you've very clearly always done, which I love. What are you looking for now that the business has exceeded your initial goals and continues to grow year on year? Do you map out big plans, as we traditionally did in business? How do you forward plan what you're doing now?

Each November we plan for the following year, and we only map out a year. I don't have a three-year vision or a five-year vision of what DSOA will look like. Because I don't need to, which is a great luxury to have.

With an online business we get to create what we want at any moment in time. I think what I love most is that my version of success can change every year. One year I can decide on a target of doubling our business. The next year I can say, let's aim for just 10 per cent growth and focus on our systems and processes. Or I want to explore a new idea over here, and I only want to put five hours a week into DSOA. Every year has changed and shifted, and we keep growing, and I want us always to keep growing because if you're not growing, you're dying. But I'm also open to new opportunities.

I also say no very often now—more than I say yes. I used to be a yes person: I'd speak at every event, accept every interview request. I'd do it all. Now I just say no. I just do the things I really want to do. I'm not worried about offending people. I'm really in tune with what a successful life looks like for me, sharing that with the people around me, and helping others understand what a successful life looks like for them. I'm more about making that happen than trying to please everyone else.

With the COVID-19 pandemic, online business has seen huge growth in terms of people packaging their expertise and sharing it with the world. Where do you think that's going to go?

One thing I know for sure is that more people are turning to the internet to create income opportunities and ways to generate revenue. Unfortunately, though, there are a lot of people out there who just make something up and put it online and sell it. That isn't really adding value to the world. I think what will happen is we'll continue to see this rise in people producing and selling their work online, but then that bubble will burst. We've seen some of that this year. COVID forced people to either lead or hide. The leaders who stepped up, who guided their communities, who led their customers — they're doing incredibly well. Those people who found it too hard are out of business, or close to it.

What lies at the heart of your success? Standing up and leading your community, sharing something obviously of massive value? Is there anything else you would say?

I think that at the core it has to be about delivering value but also solutions to your customers, and you have to care. I care deeply about the work we produce and obsess over our customer experience, which is also very important. Someone asked me the other day, if DSOA went away tomorrow, how would you feel? I would feel disappointed, because I feel like this is my life's work. But I also know that at my core I'm a teacher, and that will never go away. I will always find ways to teach and encourage and share, and hopefully inspire and motivate. So I'm not emotionally attached to my business, but I care deeply about the people we serve, and I know that if this all went away tomorrow I would go and build something new. I know that to be true.

Part V
Welcome to the new world

22

Manage your money: cash flow vs profit

Last year I was listening to a podcast of a course creator I'd been following (let's call her Renee), who was talking about her most recent course launch, which made $300 000. Wowsers, an impressive number by anyone's standards. But in business, top-line revenue doesn't mean anything if you're not keeping a careful watch on your profit levels and maintaining healthy, sustainable margins. From that $300 000, $30 000 went straight out in taxes, $170 000 on Facebook ads, $20 000 on extra software (she wasn't using Kajabi) and $20 000 on customer service support for all the extra load. That left $60 000 profit, which was still crazily impressive for a launch, a return that anyone would be grateful for, but it didn't reflect the work Renee had put in and it wasn't sustainable. That $60 000 profit on a $297 product meant more than 1000 new clients, a lot to support on an ongoing basis. Renee deserved way more profit for serving so many people.

I had a client who did content marketing and a webinar launch to her client base, selling her $997 course to 72 new clients, to produce revenue of $71 784 from the launch. Nowhere near Renee's impressive-sounding $300k launch, but she had to pay taxes of just $7180 and nothing more. She made slightly more profit than Renee made on her big launch. Not only that, but who do you think has the easier business to run — the one serving a thousand people or the one serving 72?

Remember, revenue is for vanity. Profit is for sanity. Cash flow is reality.

Cash flow is reality

I am all for a scalable and leveraged business that creates millions of dollars a year. That is totally a reality for you. I want you to start as you mean to continue and to build your business in a way that creates profit for you, rather than you completely working your arse off and having nothing left at the end of each month. There are plenty of course creators making healthy profit margins. Much of what you will do in your first 12 to 24 months will be experimental, as you test the different levers to get that balance right. People talk about online courses as passive income — they're not. They require leveraged effort, but they offer a beautiful return on investment if set up sustainably for a business that suits your lifestyle goals and financial aspirations.

You can set up your course and think you're done and you'll hit live and sit back and collect your dollars. Sorry to burst your bubble but you'd be setting yourself up for a big disappointment. Look, if you're Jennifer Lopez and you create a course on dance and then have a team member launch it and share it a couple of times on social media, yeah, that's a different story. But if you don't have the profile and reach of J.Lo, with everything you touch deservedly turning to gold, then you've got to build yourself a business around your course. Your course on its own is not a business. It is the product and one component of your business. To be successful in online education, you need to build a business around your course and really get to know your numbers.

Starting out in business I wasn't great with numbers. (I'd done basic maths at high school and had just scraped by.) I operated on the principle that if I had cash in the bank, I knew I could spend and if I didn't, then no spending. When so many dollars started flowing in and out, I knew I had to get good at managing money if I had any chance of having some left over.

What does it actually cost to run an online education business?

I don't want you to read about passive income and think you're doing something wrong. It costs money to run a high-growth business that's going to bring in millions of dollars. There are of course different ways to run your online business, and much will depend on the speed with which you want to grow, your appetite for risk and also your personal profile. Renee's $300000 launch may have paid off. Getting all that exposure may have meant that her next launch didn't require as much investment in advertising to get the same result, because by then she had word-of-mouth from all the clients who'd had a great experience with her first course.

I prefer to finance business through profit, not debt. It means you won't have your creativity stifled by the panic of not being able to make repayments, and that you'll be able to make decisions that focus on the longevity of the business rather than out of short-term desperation. The road can be a bit slower, but it means that in a couple of years you attain your million dollar business, knowing it's built on rock-solid foundations and will be around for as long as you want it to be.

Working with the cash flow pie

In my business I use a cash flow pie (see figure 5, overleaf). I keep an eye on my numbers and at the end of every month I cross-check my expenses against my allocation from the cash flow pie and adjust for the following month accordingly. This means that as my business grows, so does the amount I can invest in other areas of the business. Because we all have different lifestyle goals, your pie may look very different from mine, but it's a simple system that has enabled me to keep my business healthy.

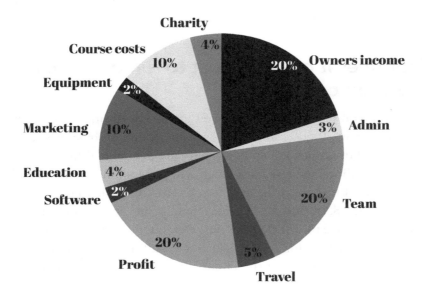

Figure 5: My expenses cash flow pie

These are the proportions in which I allocate the cash for the following month based on the previous month's performance after all taxes have been taken out:

- **20% owner's income.** Take an income from your business right from the start. Even if you only make $1000, that $200 is yours. The psychological advantage of your business giving you an income is worth it. No matter how small, you will feel rewarded. Traditionally in small business, when expenses need to be cut, the first thing to go is the owner's income. Women especially get into this habit, partly because traditionally they weren't the family's sole breadwinner so their earnings were less valued. Pay yourself like you need it.

I recommend you also create a similar pie for your personal expenses to ensure you are always allocating money into your investments, savings and expenses, using your business as a tool to fund your future personal goals.

- **20% profit.** Depending on how you do your accounting, sometimes the owner's income and profit will be combined. It's important always to retain a profit buffer for the health and sustainability of your business.

- **20% team.** This proportion will occasionally push out, especially when you make a new hire. It's a beautiful indicator of where to set your team expenses and when your business can and should hire another team member to share the load. When you're starting out and looking to hire your first team member, and you have $300 a week to allocate to the team, that's what you can spend on your contractors or your part-time personal assistant, then as your revenue grows you can afford to hire more help. The team allocation covers everything to do with team, not just their hourly rate. You also need to take into account the recruitment costs, training, educational courses, insurances and equipment. Usually your cash flow will blow out when you account for the $30 an hour for a wage but miss all of the associated costs.

- **10% marketing.** It is *very* easy to overspend on marketing. Having this allocation means at the end of the month you can look at your marketing expenses and if they were below 10 per cent of revenue after tax, you can up your spend the following month, or if they were above, you need to rein them in. This figure will always blow out in a live launch period. So if you're doing a live launch four times a year, it may be better to do your allocation over 90 days of income, knowing you'll spend the bulk of that across a 30-day launch period. Marketing covers everything to do with promoting the business, including your website, graphic design, affiliate fees, promotional materials and ads.

- **10% course costs.** As you grow your business that 10 per cent will often shrink and you'll be able to add more to your profit or your income. If you are running a straight-up self-paced course, it isn't going to cost anything to deliver. If you have a membership (as I do), then you'll definitely spend every cent of that 10 per cent. It includes conferences, live workshops, guest speaker fees, events, gifts, welcome packs and resources produced for your course.

- **5% travel.** In a normal year I will be on a plane every two or three weeks as I run live workshops and speak at events at different locations and travel around the world to inspirational conferences. If left to my own whim, I could totally spend all my profits on travel. Hello gorgeous houses of Palm Springs! It's vital for me to have a budget when it comes to travel, so I know what I can say yes to and what I need to either say no to or figure out how I can increase my revenue in order to cover it.

- **4% charity.** Your wealth can do so much good in the world. I believe that we're in this world to make a positive difference and that the more you give, the more you get. At the end of each quarter, 4 per cent of revenue goes to the various charities we support. Some are ongoing, like our educational scholarships for girls in Kenya; others are sporadic, as at Christmas time when we supply Christmas gifts to children staying in local shelters. Contributing to something that's bigger than yourself will encourage you when you feel like you can't push on. When you don't want to do that Facebook live or sell from that webinar, knowing what your success is doing for others will spur you on to get over yourself and go for it.

- **4% education.** I have had a business coach since my very first year in business. Over my 16 years in business I have spent close to $600000 on education. That may make some readers fall off their seats, thinking, 'Sheesh, you could have bought a house with that!' But here's the thing, if I hadn't invested in my own education, I wouldn't be even close to the goals I hit now. Education is a shortcut to success. Find people who are already doing what you want to do and learn from them.

I spend 4 per cent of profit on my education every single year, and still need to maintain total discipline to not go over that, because there are so many wonderful opportunities to learn in this world, especially now the web has made everything so accessible. As an example, over the past year I have purchased seven short courses. I have a private business coach and am part of two ongoing Mastermind membership programs. It keeps me inspired, gives me new ideas and of course keeps me connected with other people who have big dreams.

- **3% administration.** Ah, the boring stuff that keeps the wheels turning. Like course costs, the more your revenue, the lower this percentage will go, with the remainder converted into more profits. This includes your office if you have one, or the portion of expenses you can attribute to your home office. It's the catch-all category for power, internet, insurances and the like.

- **2% equipment.** I gave you the course creator's resource list earlier and once you've bought all of that, you shouldn't need much else. But I know that's unrealistic! You'll lust after a better microphone or the latest camera or the new super-computer with all the cool stuff. Speaking from experience, it's ridiculous how excited I got when the new MacBook Pro came out with the touch bar, and how I proceeded to purchase the most expensive computer of my life, only to find I never actually use the touch bar. Limit your equipment expenditure so you can resist the marketing hype impelling you to buy all the latest wonderful gimmickry you never knew you needed. Because you most likely don't need it. This allocation also includes your car, filming and podcasting equipment, and all the big stuff you need to power your business.

- **2% software.** This will also drop as you grow, as it's a fixed portion and once you've got it covered you won't need to add anything.

Now let's look at an example. Say you earn $10 000 a month on average in your first year as an online course creator. That means that each month, you can incur the following expenses:

- 20% owner's income = $2000

- 20% profit = $2000

- 20% team = $2000

- 10% marketing = $1000

- 10% course costs = $1000

- 5% travel = $500

- 4% charity = $400

- 4% education = $400

- 3% administration = $300

- 2% equipment = $200

- 2% software = $200

If you're running a million dollar-a-year business, your figures change to a monthly spend of:

- 20% owner's income = $16 666

- 20% profit = $16 666

- 20% team = $16 666

- 10% marketing = $8333

- 10% course costs $8333

- 5% travel = $4166

- 4% charity = $3333

- 4% education = $3333

- 3% administration = $2499

- 2% equipment = $1666

- 2% software = $1666

One of the main reasons I love working with my cash flow pie is that I can see how quickly my money is allocated. Without conscious allocation, your cash flow (like your time) will be spent on all sorts of things and just dissipate. This allows you to allocate your profits in line with your values and to grow your wealth consistently over time.

As your business grows, pay attention to your money beliefs and what makes you feel comfortable and safe. The resources section at the back lists some great books and courses written and run by very smart people who specialise in finance. One of the habits that keeps me disciplined is every morning when I get to my desk I log in to my banking portal and check all the balances and all the transactions and make sure I didn't do any mindless spending. You might think that someone who runs a million dollar business shouldn't be spending time worrying about an extra $50 here or there, but the reason I know that I will be able to live a comfortable life into retirement is that I have watched those dollars and cents and consciously invested them. You can't manage what you don't know, so learn to know and love your numbers.

I think people who declare 'Money doesn't buy you happiness' have never truly been poor. You can go to my first book if you want to know my full backstory. In it, I speak about how I got started in business and how I created my dream life from nothing. I have known what it's like to have to put food back at the grocery checkout because I'd gone over budget. I've known what it feels like to go through the essential bills and have to come up with a strategy to pay them in a certain order so services wouldn't be disconnected. I've had to vacate my home when

I couldn't afford to live there anymore. I have known the pain of being poor, and I'll take wealth any day. Having more than enough money gives you choices, freedom and so much opportunity. I want that for you. It's there for the taking. There is an infinite amount of money in the world and it's continually being printed and circulated. Find your own special blend of how you're going to serve the world *and* be financially compensated, then how you're going to spend your money to live the life you choose for the rest of your days.

Action step

Think about how you'll choose to allocate your money, then create your own expenses pie.

23
Say no to protect your energy

Starting a business is full on! When you start your online education business you'll be set on your path, but then you'll look to the side and think you need to jump on over there and do what that person is doing, or maybe that person ahead of you. You'll find yourself being pulled in different directions and getting nowhere fast. Trying to do everything and be all things to all people leads inevitably to burnout, and then you're just as useless as the 'g' in lasagne.

This may be your first business or perhaps you've had others. But no matter how many times you've done it, when you create something new and put it out into the world, it's a big thing. It's about how much work it takes but also the emotional weight of it. Looking at what we have to do from a practical standpoint is so easy. We just have to do one thing then the next, making sure we're focusing our time and energy on the tasks that will yield the greatest results. Emotionally, we can psych out and feel overwhelmed and exhausted, sometimes even just by the thought of the road ahead!

It's vitally important to keep healthy, both emotionally and physically. Depending on our natural habits, this is easier said than done. When there's so much to do, and you love your work, it can be very easy to fall into the trap of overworking. I have tried all types of work routines. I tried the 5 am club (eek! I did not love it). I have done nothing but work, sleep and eat, and I have tried a more balanced approach. Now I can say with 100 per cent certainty that by slowing down, you will speed up. Your work will suffer from workaholic tendencies and you won't even realise it. It can feel very frustrating and counterproductive to take a break when you have so much you want to do. But when you do, you will come back firing! Your brain will be fresh and energised, you'll have amazing ideas and unstoppable self-belief, and you'll take on the world like the champion you are.

Mental health is such an issue in our modern world as we take on unrealistic expectations of performance and desires. Looking after your mental health does not make you weak, it makes you smart. No one can benefit from burning out and added mental stress. Starting and growing a business—hell, life in general—is stressful enough. It's incredibly important that you consciously monitor your mental state and learn to work with your natural tendencies and do whatever it is you need to do to help yourself. Often when someone isn't experiencing the progress that they would like, it's because they're battling against their own emotional and mental demons. Befriend your mind, and work with it to get the results you want. Working with your mind and body in harmony and feeling the work flow from you is one of the greatest feelings. Figuring out your own unique equilibrium that empowers you to find your flow more quickly will become your absolute superpower. If you see others performing well and showing a lot of energy, it's because they've figured out what works for them and just unapologetically go with it.

My good friend Keri knows she needs regular baths to calm her mind and body, and she'll luxuriate in that tub for as long as she wants to recharge, so when she's in service to others she has so much more to give. Another friend has incredibly painful periods and used to push through it because she didn't want to lose that productive time, but she found that suffering through the headaches and nausea and all that came with it meant she was spending five to seven days putting out substandard work. Now she takes two complete days off, lies in bed or in the sunshine reading and allowing her body to heal, then comes back to work ready to go. By befriending her body she has done what it needs and her mind is rewarding her for it.

Don't get me started on women's disadvantage as a result of hormonal imbalances and how much that can impact our work! If you are affected, monitor it and work with it. Taking a break and resting when your body and mind needs you to will mean you have so much more to give in the long term. It will help you create a sustainable business rather than putting in a year and then giving up, as so many aspiring entrepreneurs do.

Before you embark on your new business career, make a list of all the things that keep you mentally healthy—I call it my 'happy list'—and ensure you do at least one thing from the list every day. If I catch myself with raised cortisol levels and shallow breathing, I whip out that list and go straight into the easiest thing on there that can reset my state.

Here's my list for some inspiration:

- Soak in a bubble bath.

- Swim in the ocean.

- Take a walk on the beach or in the bush.

- Recline in my reading chair with a fabulous novel.

- Watch a romantic comedy.

- Have sex.

- Go to lunch with friends.

- Dance and sing.

- Play a game (netball or tennis).

- Do a yoga class.

- Spend an hour in a float tank.

- Take one of my children on a special date and give them my undivided attention.

- Potter around the garden.

- Play a family game of cards.

- Write in my journal.

- Go full woowoo with my crystals and tarot cards.

- Go out for a fancy meal with Mat.

- Play with my dog.

Create your own happy list so you have a process in place to remind you that it can't all be about work. You need a wide range of activities to create joy in your heart and keep that creativity flowing.

One of the greatest superpowers in business is maintaining your energy level and an optimistic outlook. As I've said before, often it's not the technical challenges but our unhealthy habitual behaviours that block us. Developing mental toughness prevents us from psyching out when it gets hard. If you commit to your goals, you have to be willing to do what it takes to get there. There's no point in saying 'I want to make a million dollars' if you're not prepared to do the work. Keeping your mind healthy will give you the best chance of backing yourself and cheering yourself on as you enter the arena.

Protecting your energy levels is something you'll have to master as you grow your business. When you start out, you're in the mode of YES! If an opportunity arises, you take it. In your first 12 months you're trying to get some runs on the board, to build your reputation and get some all-important cash in the door. You do what you have to do in order to do what you want to do. But what gets you to the first level won't get you to the next. The reason so many business owners reach a point of burnout and plateaued business growth is they haven't switched from saying yes to saying no. You're not superhuman, and nor should you want to be. There comes a point when you will need to recognise that you're running around like a crazy person doing what others want you to do, and you need to switch to saying no to protect your energy. No more doing work for free. No more sessions where people can 'pick your brain'. No more under-charging for your services. You decide on your boundaries, then stick to them.

For business owners, especially those of us who are people pleasers, this is *hard*. We naturally want to help people and to serve, and that can be confused with being at everyone's beck and call, and with your willingness to help being abused. The most difficult part of saying no is you don't want to be perceived as an arsehole. This is where you must circle back to your values and remind yourself what you're doing and why you're doing it. You're not running a charity, you're running a business. Yes, you want to serve people, and that's the very reason your business exists, but you serve the people who value your services and pay for the privilege. For everyone else, it's a no.

When you're asked to do things for free, or you have to say no to clients because you're fully committed, the best policy is always honesty. Here are some examples of how to say no:

- Thank you for thinking of me. As my time is so limited, I can only commit to paid work. If you'd like to see the options to work with me, please click here: [LINK].

- Thank you so much for reaching out. Out of respect for my paying clients, I'm unable to give detailed advice across email/ social media. Here's where you can book a consultation: [LINK], or my course is here: [LINK]. You'll also find loads of free resources to help you out on my website and podcast. I look forward to working with you further soon and seeing you fly!

- This sounds like such an interesting opportunity. Thank you for referring me! Here's where you can find the information for the current services I offer: [LINK]. I think [COURSE] would be the best fit for [person referred].

- I'm so happy to hear you're loving the course! Out of respect for my private clients, I am unable to give detailed specific coaching to course participants. If you'd like to book a consultation, then I can give you my undivided attention to help you elevate. You can book that here: [LINK].

The only time honesty is not the best option is when you have a potential client who you know is not going to respect your boundaries or your time. With those energy-suckers, you need to politely decline and back away. It's tempting to say yes to all clients, but if you're serving them on a group or individual level and they're not the right fit, they can affect the energy of the entire group as well as yours. To preserve the culture you work so hard to build in your business, you need to be able to say no.

There are many parts of this business that require so much of you. Preserve your value and your energy. Protect your energy as though it's the most important asset of the business, because it actually is.

Action step

Create your own 'happy list'.

24
Design life your way

Hands down the greatest gift of your online course business (other than its scalability) is your ability to work from wherever you want in the world. I've run coaching calls from the Gobi Desert in Mongolia and from a beachside shack on the island of Madagascar. Now I do it from a purpose-built pink cottage on our property that I made into my office.

You can design your way of work however you want. If you want to go to an office every day, you can rent one or share a co-working space. If you want to work from home, you can do that. If you want to travel, you can do it from the back of your van as you journey across the country. The internet is accessible pretty much everywhere now. All you need is your filming equipment, a laptop and wifi and you're good to go.

Over a decade ago, Tim Ferriss wrote one of my absolute favourite books, *The 4-Hour Workweek*, where he floated the idea of running a sustainable business that gives you a regular income while you vagabond around the world. It lit such a fire in me that I've been living partly nomadically ever since.

To me, it makes zero sense to spend hours every day commuting to the office. The only advantage of offices is the social connection, but you can get that outside of your work so easily. If you commute to an office 30 minutes from your home, that's 120 hours a year that you're losing on your commute. That's crazy! That's 12 whole days of waking hours that you get back when you remove the commute. You can work wherever and whenever you like.

It is drummed into us from an early age that success depends on hard work and hustle! Creating a high-growth million dollar micro business does not depend on your being trapped behind your computer to slog out long days while you live on bad food, coffee and alcohol. The success of your micro business depends on your being able to distinguish the important from the unimportant, and to work strategically on those activities that create the biggest results in the shortest amount of time.

One of the great lessons I took from my round-the-world trip was the insight that many of the beliefs we adopt unquestioningly don't represent absolute truth; they're culturally ingrained. Every culture has a body of established truths that are generally treated as incontestable fact, but these truths can vary widely, even irreconcilably, across different cultures. A work week based on 40 hours, from 9 am to 5 pm, five days a week, is no more than a cultural construct. Who even decided that Saturday and Sunday constituted the weekend? Why should we feel guilty if we take Monday off because it's a 'work day'? All of these rules we live our lives by are social constructs that we can choose to accept or reject. If you love the 9 to 5, then stick with it. But if you want to work irregular hours around your surfing schedule, then why not?

So many people sit at their desk doing absolutely nothing productive, but they have to sit there because it's not 'knock-off time' yet. If we had the discipline to work in blocks of time that best suit our own body clock and preferences and when we get in-flow, we could be so much more productive. If you're a morning person, work from 5 am until lunchtime and call it a day. If you're a night person, you can work late. If you have kids, work around that. You can do whatever you want!

Think of when you're going on holiday and suddenly everything at work becomes so urgent. You feel like you have to get all these loose ends tied up before your two-week vacation or ... the world just might actually implode. So you work your tail off and break land speed records to get it all done in time. What if you always worked like that? For most people working 9 to 5, it wouldn't be sustainable to keep up that pace for so long without a break. But if you took that level of urgency, specificity and productivity, worked in 90-minute blocks, then rested with some activity from your happy list, and you did that for three to four days a week, I bet you would actually get better results in 20 hours of work than you would from your usual 40.

If you don't believe me, run the experiment. To do it, you do have to plan it and be disciplined, which means you don't waste time faffing around. When you feel 'on', you work. When you feel 'off', you don't. So when you're on, you absolutely go for it. You know exactly the things in your business you need to work on to get the result. You're not doing busy work, you're doing results-driven work.

It no longer makes sense to be stuck in one place and only have a few weeks off each year. You can design your work life so you can turn the tap on and off as you need and want. Some of the world's top course creators are doing one major course launch a year. Of course there's a lot to do in between, with creating content and delivering their services, but all of these activities can be batched, then you have all this freedom when you get to do whatever you want. I wouldn't recommend doing one launch a year until you're well past the million mark so you can keep that momentum going, but even with three or four a year, you'll be able to take weeks or months off and do what you need to do from wherever you are. If you love to be home, then by all means stay at home, but just find something outside of work to keep you stimulated so you can maintain your enthusiasm for what you're building and enjoy the fruits of your labour rather than working all the time.

The lifestyle choices are all yours. You get to choose where, how, when and with whom you work. I mostly like to have people with me as I find the direct communication much more effective than with a VA and we can get a lot more done in less time when we're together. With my children in high school now, we're not travelling as a family as much as we used to, which means I can fall into overworking all too easily. I used to use travel as my way to disconnect and take a break, so I've had to reinvent those habits.

Instead of doing a 'normal' five-day work week, now my team do three big days (Monday to Wednesday) in the office with me, Thursday is a work-from-home day, then a three-day weekend, but with a quick 30-minute check-in on Friday to make sure there's nothing urgent that needs attention. For me it means I work three big days, which I absolutely love, then have four days off. This way both my employees and I have a nice break and a chance to recharge for the week to come.

Some of these weeks I will create video or record podcasts because I'm feeling inspired, but it means I have the freedom to choose each day what I feel like doing. If I'm in the garden tending my vegetables on a Sunday and I get a stroke of inspiration, you bet I'm going to run into my studio and hit record on that podcast episode. Each month I also take a week off, when I can choose to go away or hang out at home or at work. What I've learned is that without those breaks and without that freedom, the inspiration doesn't come with the same strikes of awesomeness—it's more forced.

My goal is maximum productivity and results. I want to have an impact on thousands of people on this planet, and to achieve what those people need and deserve that I give them my best. They're not paying me to show up tired and drained. I'm being paid to solve problems and propose creative new ideas for their business growth—and for that I need to feel sharp and energised. Look, I'm taking a break because my clients need me to! Isn't that the best business set-up ever?

What do your audience, your loved ones and your heart need from you?

Action step

Create your goals for both your business and your lifestyle, then go chase them!

25
Where to from here?

You, my darling friend, are ready to launch. There are many ways to launch an online course. The way I recommend you start with is both the simplest and the one that will get you the best results.

You want to be able to have fun at your first launch, because this life is supposed to be fun. Try to keep it simple and keep it light. You'll need to, because the first time you launch you'll be scared shitless! While it's a super-low financial investment, you will have put a lot of yourself into it. You'll have stepped way outside of your comfort zone. You'll be worried about being judged by friends, family and especially yourself. This is not the time to back away and play it safe. If you truly want success, this is the time to dive in and give it everything you've got.

A launch, done right, is full on. You're highly engaged with your team and your community and showing up in all the places you need to with lots of energy and crystal-clear messaging.

In the lead-up to your launch be prepared to show yourself, embracing who you are and owning the expertise and credibility you have. Know that you can do this, that all the ideas you've had for your life while you've been reading this book are totally possible for you.

A million dollar business means $83 333 a month, $19 230 a week, $2739 a day. They can seem like absurdly big numbers at the start, but with time you'll come to see that it can be done. From the example of the successful course creators I've worked with, it's entirely realistic to expect to achieve that level within two or three years of starting. The key is to sustain your efforts for at least 18 months with as much enthusiasm as you had on day one. You'll get the results if you persist until you achieve them.

Now, to recap, to prepare for launch you needed to work your way through the following steps:

1. Create a brand that you love.

2. Do your fear-setting exercise.

3. Make your transformation promise crystal clear.

4. Know your vision.

5. Set up your business and protect your IP.

6. Create your course.

7. Set up your pricing.

8. Create your webinar.

9. Establish your content marketing.

10. Run a practice webinar.

11. Get comfortable on camera.

12. Create your systems and procedures as you go.

13. Hire your team.

14. Create your launch plan.

15. Create your client onboarding and ongoing service plan.

16. Set your goals.

17. GO!

Throughout this book I've shown you how you can cover each of these steps. If you've read it in one hit, now's the time to go back to the beginning, and this time create as you go. Use this book as a handbook and guide to bringing your business to life.

Your first launch is one of the most valuable learning experiences you'll ever have. As the energy and anticipation builds, you will become increasingly amped. Clear your space and your time when you're ready to go. Everything that can be pre-scheduled should be. You need complete focus to give this the attention it deserves. Don't find yourself writing the social media posts and emails on the day they're going out. All of that needs to be done well ahead, so when you're in launch mode all your energy is directed towards connecting with clients. Clear your inbox before you start and clear your schedule of day-to-day activities. Allow nothing else to interrupt or distract you in launch week.

When you hit live and send your course out into the world, your nerves will be out of control. Gosh, even I still feel nervous at a major launch! You'll check your emails like a woman possessed, watching sales coming in and getting so excited as you welcome another person into your course. Each one of these transactions represents the faith they've put in you and what you've created. You need to recognise this and send them a message of love and recognition. You will spend much of your launch welcoming people, promoting on social media, answering people's questions and comments, and thanking people for sharing. You will go through periods of exhaustion, which is why I have emphasised the need to be well prepared to ensure you have the energy you need.

Be really kind to yourself. Be patient and remember that this is a marathon, not a sprint. Your first launch may feel so far from your million dollar dream, but the launch itself is an incredible achievement. It will teach you so much about what you need to know, what needs changing and tweaking, and how to get your messaging even clearer to attract your perfect client.

Unless you're from outer space or a hard-core narcissist, you will feel the fear of being under the spotlight. This can hold you back more than anything else. People surveyed have said that they would rather die than step onto a stage to speak publicly! Your fears will threaten to undo you …

What if they don't like me?

What if they think I'm too fat?

What if they see that scar on my face?

What if they think I'm ugly?

What if they don't think I'm smart enough?

What if nobody shows up?

What if no one buys my course?

What if they hate my clothes?

What if I sound annoying?

What if I freeze or say the wrong thing?

What if I make a fool of myself?

What if I'm just not good enough?

What if? There are so many fears you could fall victim to. But what if you recognise them and break through and do it anyway? What if you feel that uncertainty in the pit of your stomach and *do it anyway*? What if your wildest dreams come true and you become your own champion? Choose life! Choose to be one of the few brave enough to step up and truly shine. Then you can encourage others to do the same.

Yesterday I took a break from writing and went out on a friend's boat. I grew up with boats and used to water-ski and wakeboard every weekend—I absolutely loved the free feeling of zooming around on the water. But then I stopped for two years while I had my babies. When I finally got back on the water behind a boat I went to step off the pontoon onto my ski as I had hundreds of times before. I stepped off the platform, the boat accelerated and I slipped. I'm not sure what or how it happened, but the front of the wooden ski shot up and hit me right between the eyes, splitting open and breaking my nose. I found myself treading water in a growing pool of blood and in a state of shock. It was two years before I tried it again. This time there was no jumping off the pontoon—I was going to take a safer start from the deep water and let the boat pull me up.

The boat took off with a roar and I held on grimly, determined to overcome my fear and stand tall. I gripped the rope while I was being pulled through the water but couldn't stand up. I tried again and again and again, and each time the rope was ripped out of my hands and I was unable to hold on. By the time I admitted defeat, my hands were raw and shaking. I cried with frustration and disappointment.

That was eight years ago. Yesterday I sat nervously on the boat wondering whether to try again. I knew that if I succeeded I would feel so empowered, on top of the world. But I also knew that if I failed I would not only feel humiliated in front of my family and friends, but more than anything I would be disappointed in myself. I ran through the fear-setting exercise in my head and decided the possible upside was worth risking the potential downside. I was in a safe space, and no one on that boat would have thought less of me if I failed. They just wanted me to give it a try. I strapped the wakeboard onto my feet feeling my heart beating heavily and the nerves in the pit of my stomach.

In my mind I ran through a visualisation of the boat taking off, with me holding strong and standing tall. I felt what it would feel like to do it perfectly. And I jumped in.

Once I was ready, I looked expectantly at Mat, the only one who knew what this actually meant to me. He just smiled calmly, looking like he already totally knew I would nail it. I yelled out, 'Yep, ready!' and tightened my grip, looked at my body and told it we could do this. The boat took off ... and up I popped. Straight to the top of the water, like that old fear had never been there. I skimmed across the water feeling the spray hit my face and feeling like I could do anything in the world I truly wanted to.

I share this story because we all feel like there's things in life that are just not for us. Like there are things accessible to others but not on the cards for us. If you have the desire in your heart to do something, you owe it to yourself to try. You will never feel like you're truly capable of something until it's done. The only person it's important to prove yourself to is you. Every time you find yourself doing something you were unsure you would be able to do, it will give you a little more confidence in yourself, which will then fuel you to go on and try something else. That momentum will build, and before you know it you'll be stepping onto that stage with the spotlight on you. Your heart will be beating like a drum, but because you've stepped up and proved it to yourself hundreds of times in little ways before, you know you're going to be fine. You know you're safe to try because you've tried so many things before. Don't hold back from trying that next little thing. It could well be that the world is waiting for that very thing you have in your head right now.

Our 'what if' fears are all about us, and this is actually a selfish way of looking at things, because this launch is really not about us at all. It's about the people we serve and the impact we can have on others. Don't make it about you—focus on those you're helping and what you can do for them.

Think of your first launch, and the subsequent ones, as an experiment, and know that not only will you achieve your goals, but the journey will bring you more than you could ever imagine. The only way this doesn't work is if you don't do the work. You'll learn so much about yourself and about the world. You'll enrich your human experience on this earth simply by daring to have a go.

Be proud of yourself for committing to a life less ordinary and being bold enough to design your life on your terms while committing to living a life of service to others. Trust in the process, think about the clients you're serving, listen to your heart and follow your joy. Know that if you do this, your life will be quite different in the years to come. Your current circumstances do not determine your future. Never underestimate what you are capable of and who you are capable of becoming.

You're creating something that will give you a level of freedom denied so many in this world. You will be one of the few lucky ones who get to do what they love and get paid well for doing it. You can use your wealth to make a difference in your community and in the world, and make your life count.

I am incredibly happy for you. I'm so grateful that you've trusted me on this journey, and I can't wait to receive that email from you about your new course and your first launch! I believe in you and your dreams and I know you're about to prove to yourself just how awesome your life can be.

Dream big, plan well and take massive action.

SUCCESS STORY

Denise Duffield-Thomas
Chillpreneur

Denise Duffield-Thomas is the money mentor for the new wave of online entrepreneurs who want to make money and change the world. She helps women charge premium prices, release their fear of money and create first-class lives. Her books Get Rich, Lucky Bitch! *and* Chillpreneur *give a fresh and funny roadmap to living a life of abundance without burnout. Her Money Bootcamp course has helped over 6000 students from all around the world. She's a lazy introvert and an unbusy mother of three. She owns a rose farm and lives by the beach in sunny Australia.*

We talked over Zoom in early December 2020.

How has the growth of your online business worked out?

The first year it was $60 000, doing one-to-one coaching, then it was $120 000, $250 000, $500 000, $750 000, $1.2 million, $1.7 million, $2.5 million, $3 million … I pretty much doubled it every year in the first years and hit $1.2 million about five years ago. Obviously, I haven't doubled every year since then. Some of that is a bit deliberate, too.

I remember my friend Natalie McNeil talking about this. She was like, 'Oh, next year, I'm going to take a year where I don't launch as much. I'm going to build some systems behind the scenes'. I thought, 'You're *allowed* to do that?' I think because I've never been that motivated by numbers for numbers' sake, it has to be really sustainable for me. I want to make sure that nothing really stresses me or the team out. We've been tempted to go in slightly different directions. But I always pull it back to the core of what we do and how can we make this really, really simple and easy, so it doesn't create extra stress for anybody.

Have there been times that you've deliberately put the brakes on, when you've seen an opportunity come up and you've thought, you know what, if I go in this direction, we'll grow too fast. Or have you always said yes to growth?

One decision we made about two years ago was to let go of our affiliate program. It was bringing in lots of sales, but it was creating increasing stress. I've always followed Marie Forleo's kind of business model. She had a tonne of affiliates, but she's stopped hers now too. So two years ago, Mark (my husband) was doing the affiliate program, and what I noticed was that many people needed a lot of hand holding. It became another customer group for us, where they needed training. Basically, unpaid customer service and unpaid mentorship. People saying, for example, 'Oh, I forgot to put my link in, can you figure out which sales are mine?'

We had people complaining about having to pay PayPal fees on their affiliate stuff, even though I had paid them when I received the income. People are just clueless about marketing, to be honest, and are so demanding, 'Where do I do this? How do I do this?' We saw all of the work that was going into that group, even though it was bringing in income—I'm always thinking how can we get the same or better results with less work—so we decided to put the money into ads instead.

At the peak of that program, we were paying out $600 000 that year, which meant we were making $600 000. But it was taking a lot of time. We were getting to the point that I thought we're going to have to hire someone just to do this, just for training, which is what Marie Forleo did. She had at least one full-time person creating stuff, dealing with all the complaints, training, holding people's hands, even sending out the emails. So I thought, let's just ditch this. I knew if we'd continued to grow it, it would have been, you know, millions more dollars for us, but it just wasn't the way I like to grow my business. I thought, what would happen if we invested $600000 in ads? We've done two launches without it, and we've had amazing launches. Not necessarily heaps more revenue, but heaps more profit.

How do you deal with the comparison trap?

I think the lifetime access model is very flawed. A story on that: A friend of mine gave her people a year's notice that the course was closing down on a lifetime access program. She has had more complaints about that than about anything else she's ever done in her career. She's had someone threaten to sue her. Even though she gave them a year's notice, when no additional people were joining, no additional income for her, customer service, hosting all the staff—and someone's actually threatening to sue her over it!

One thing that helped me was flipping the situation in my mind—like, well, if they can do it, I can do it. A friend of mine, Leonie Dawson, the first couple of years she was always ahead of me income wise. But I used that as motivation, because I'd say, 'Oh my god, Mark, she's making $30000 in a month'. She's always been very honest and open about that kind of stuff publicly.

You know, I make 10 times more than that now. But you can use comparison to inspire you or to cripple you. I've always used it to inspire me. What helps, too, is realising that so many people are doing so many different things. Someone just needs to hear it in your language. You obviously can't copy someone directly, and it sucks when people copy you.

How have you dealt with that as you've grown?

It's annoying, huh? Most of the time I ignore it, because I know what it takes, mindset wise, to sustain a business like mine. I also know that most copycats change their business model every three to six months. I think they don't have any original ideas, or they get bored. So when I see someone do it I think, good luck with that.

In terms of growth, you're a rarity in that you've got your one signature program and that's what you sell, again and again. You've resisted the temptation to add on things in the ascension model. Did you consciously choose that as your growth strategy?

No. I have done a few different things. My first year I did one-to-one. Then I had a course called The Inspired Life Formula. The following year I did Money Bootcamp—I thought it was just going to be a one-off. Then I had a soulmate course. Then I added in Sacred Money Archetypes a couple of years ago. I decided to tinker in the top end rather than the bottom. Each time I add something new, I come back to myself and think, no, all roads lead to Bootcamp. It's still tough sometimes, because people ask me to do different things.

You have a beautiful business with a small team. How have you managed that and the time you put in?

I think I've always erred on the side of caution. So I've never gone too big and pulled it back. I've probably understaffed more than anything. And maybe that's my personality. And I suspect you're probably like that a bit too. I think, well, I can do it myself. Sometimes you're not the best person to do it, but you just think, I can't be fucked explaining this to somebody else. Then I realised, oh no, actually someone else could do this way better. Eliminate first, then automate, then batch. Outsource and get someone to batch it in a short period of time, then delegate and hire someone else. I'm in a really privileged situation here because Mark is such a great asset to the company. If I had to replace him, I'd probably have to hire five different people.

I'm not super productive with my time at all. The thing I'm smart about is figuring out what are the activities that are actually going to move the needle, and focusing on those things. For me that's podcast interviews. That's why I do three to five of them a week. Because

I know that that's going to fill up our list, that's going to give leads for Mark that will eventually lead to a Bootcamp sale.

I've found, though, that we probably do have to pitch a little bit more, because I find, again, going to the next level of best use of time, I'm like, I really need to catch listeners from bigger podcasts. That's my highest value activity. The other thing I personally do is social media content, so probably once every two or three months I'll sit down and just create a whole bunch of stuff in a day and schedule it all. They're the only two things I really do. And if you look at it, that's only a couple of hours a week really. In terms of delivery, I do two calls a month, which is about three hours. And that's it. But I'm so bad with my time. I'm such a procrastinator. It's just that I do these high-value things. So everything else is only a nice-to-have, and I just never get around to those!

Do you ever feel guilt over other people running the business while you're the face of it, and you get to do those high-value things, while everyone else keeps the cogs turning in the background?

I used to a little bit with Mark. Not so much my assistants, because I've always been very clear about hiring people who like to be behind the scenes. In the early days, I would interview people, and they would be a little mini-me, and they would last a day and would be like, 'Thanks for the ideas. I'm going to go and start my own business now'. I've always been very, very hands off, even transactional with my team. I don't know their kids' names, but I'm fair, I pay well and on time. Still, I'm the boss, I'm not their best friend. With Mark, though, when he came into the business, he had to have some re-education about the value of our respective hours. For example, he'd say, it was just an hour webinar, whereas I spent six hours doing bla bla bla, and I'm thinking, yeah, but no one's paying you to do those other things. So I kind of had to say, 'I'm the golden goose. I'm the one they pay money to come and see. Not you. So an hour of my time, I'm sorry, I don't mean to be a bitch, but it's worth a lot more than an hour of your time'. So I felt guilty, then I got angry. And now I don't feel guilty at all.

We have a part-time assistant. I had one who was with me for about five years. And we've had Mel for about two years. They're not permanent part time — they're contractors. She has other clients too. During launch times I might get people who've worked with us before.

Have you got every aspect of the business systemised so people know what to do when they come in?

Yes and no. When Mark came into the business, I was like, 'Oh shit, I need to put some stuff down on paper'. But then he had some really bad habits from corporate. He would send me an email to approve and send it as an attachment. And I was like, 'In my company it's a Google Doc. How did you do version control in corporate?' He would say, 'Oh, we just send attachments back and forth, like version 1.3, 1.5'. And I was like, 'We don't do that'. We do really simple stuff. So Google Docs for everything. When they're finished, it has to go through Grammarly. That was another thing I had to educate everyone on. They tagged me and I approved it. Our launch documents are 60 pages long, and they'll include every single email and we're pretty clear on things like the date, the subject line, when it should go out, who is programming it. That's pretty much the biggest system. My bookkeeper is an external consultant, so they've got their own system, and everything is pretty well covered. It's not like we're doing new stuff all the time, you know. The business has been pretty much the same for the last five years.

I like the batching thing. You might have one little task that you can't do, so you can get someone on Fiverr to do it. I like those little micro-outsourcing things, one for practice and two for speed and cost. And not having that ongoing expense is really key. The biggest thing I outsourced in the first year was customer service for five hours a week. I wanted regular customer service emails, because my inbox was my biggest source of stress. So I hired someone who was doing that for multiple clients already. I didn't have to come up with a system and train them, or even feel bad about hiring them for only five hours. I wanted someone who could switch easily between my inbox and their other clients' inboxes, and they were just really professional about it.

They didn't answer pretending to be me. The first two weeks we went through every email together, and I would say, this is how I would answer that. But she answered as her, not as me. So you should say, 'Hi, this is Denise's assistant Amber', and explain the answer to that particular dilemma. This is how you would find that information. And then we probably met every week for about six weeks. And the inquiries got fewer and fewer. Because it was the same thing over and over again: 'I can't access my whatever' or 'Can I interview Denise?', but it really came down to only five things. I was so concerned about how she was going to answer, I literally dictated it, but over time I came to trust her. Eventually we moved over to our own system.

On social media I just felt like I wanted a little bit more privacy. I'm re-recording Bootcamp in about two weeks, which I do every three years. I actually want the sales page and the sales video to be less about me. I don't want the business to be all about me and my success. I want it to be a bit more about that connected energy. This is about you and your success. In the last couple of years I haven't actually wanted to talk so much about transparency and numbers, which I know people really love hearing about. But I was like, it's not about me and what I've achieved, it's what I can help you achieve. So, shifting the focus and doing more picture quotes and things like that. Or if I'm sharing something personal, is this in service? Is this going to help somebody? Is this going to lead someone to my work, or is it just oversharing for the sake of it? And some people are happy to be more transparent than others. This is just one of the reasons why I wasn't as transparent this year, especially around how much money I made, even though I published my tax return. I think there's a fine line between being inspiring and being braggy and inappropriate when people are losing their jobs.

A lot of people say to me, 'Oh, this looks amazing. I think I'll start a blog'. But they just don't have the work ethic. It takes time. So here's a quote I love from my friend Jennifer Kim. She said, 'You've got to earn your chill'. I've earned my chill, I've done hundreds and hundreds of blog posts. I've done thousands of hours of sweat equity. I used to sit and do hour-long Periscopes in my car with my kids asleep. Money Bootcamp has been around for eight years. I can't even imagine how many Q&A calls I've done, how many thousands of hours I've spent in that group helping people. It takes focus, but it doesn't take as much perfection as people think. I've been half-assed but in a consistent way for a long time!

Going back to your excitement at making that $225, do you think that as we get more successful we become desensitised to those moments?

Definitely. Mark sent me a text a couple of days ago: 'I think we made perhaps $300 000 last month'. Obviously, we haven't got our bookkeeping back yet for the final number. I used to celebrate every single client. Somebody bought my ebook! Someone bought my course! I think you need that at the start, because there are so many shitty moments, so at the start you need every single good one. Now I'm just, 'Oh, that's cool'. But I have to remind myself to really celebrate other people's successes, so when somebody in our group sells their first hundred-dollar course I'm so excited because I know how hard that is.

Do you think in the beginning, when people are picking this up, they have to do the hustle and grind from the beginning? Or do you think there are now smarter ways to use automation and systems to grow?

You think of entrepreneurs starting now, and they've got payment systems, and you can do a website in a day. They don't know how lucky they are. Free marketing, it's super simple. That doesn't mean the mindset stuff is easy. I think it's just as hard as it ever was for people starting now. The results at the start are a bit slower coming. You have to believe in yourself, right? You have to back yourself, overcome your fear, work on your money mindset. You have to work on your fear of pricing.

All that stuff, I think will be as true in 10 years, 20 years, as it is now. Only the technology changes. The other thing I think people need to get is that the basics are always the same, you know. I still have to market. I have to be a storyteller. That's going to be true no matter what technology or marketing systems we have. Maybe it will be holograms beamed into people's lounge rooms, but it's always going to be about telling a story, and telling people how you can help them. That's what it's always been about. And it always, always will be.

resources

Digital resources you'll find at milliondollarmicrobusiness.com:
Budget spreadsheet
Course planning spreadsheet
Equipment links
Brand board example
Webinar checklist
Webinar content planner
Checklist for what to have on your systems manual
Downloadable happy list
Printable tables for Parts I and II
Tim Ferriss's 2017 fear-setting TED talk, 'Why you should define your fears instead of your goals'

To help with brainstorming:
Answer the Public: www.answerthepublic.com
Google Trends: trends.google.com

To check name availability:
Namecheckr: www.namecheckr.com

Register your domain name:
GoDaddy: godaddy.com

Trademark search:
Australia: ipaustralia.gov.au
USA: uspto.gov

Software:
Kajabi: kajabi.com
Stripe: stripe.com
Canva: canva.com
Monday: Monday.com
StreamYard: streamyard.com
Calendly: calendly.com
Adobe Creative Suite: adobe.com/creativecloud
Libsyn: https://libsyn.com/
Otter: otter.ai
Later: later.com
Dropbox: dropbox.com
Xero: xero.com
Quaderno: quadernoapp.com
Google Workspace: workspace.google.com
Zoom: zoom.com

To help you to design your logo:
Fiverr: fiverr.com
Upwork: upwork.com
Creative Market: creativemarket.com

To choose your brand colours:
Complimentary colour options: www.paletton.com
Trending colour palettes: www.coolors.co/palettes
Colour picking tool: www.canva.com/colors/color-wheel/
Colour combinations: www.canva.com/learn/100-color-combinations/

Some great blogs:
Seth Godin: seths.blog
Kevin Kelly: www.kk.org/thetechnium/1000-true-fans/
Marie Forleo: www.marieforleo.com/marietv

Some of the best books for course creators:
One Minute Millionaire by Mark Victor Hansen
Chillpreneur by Denise Duffield-Thomas
Unfuck Your Finances by Melissa Browne
Good to Great by Jim Collins
Radical Candor by Kim Scott
One Minute Manager by Ken Blanchard and Spencer Johnson
Rocket Fuel by Gino Wickman
Traction by Gino Wickman
The 4-hour Workweek by Tim Ferriss
Daring Greatly by Brené Brown
Pre-suasion by Robert Cialdini
Love Yourself Like Your Life Depends on It by Kamal Ravikant
Start with Why by Simon Sinek
Barking up the Wrong Tree by Eric Barker
The Subtle Art of Not Giving A Fuck by Mark Manson
High Performance Habits by Brendon Burchard (or anything by Brendon Burchard!)
Super Attractor by Gabrielle Bernstein
Breaking the Habit of Being Yourself by Joe Dispenza

Some great conferences and workshops:
SXSW
Dr John Demartini The Breakthrough Experience
Social Media Marketing World
Online Business Con with Tyler McCall
Kajabi Conference

Some great courses and thought leaders to check out:
Brendon Burchard brendon.com
Colin Boyd—Selling through webinar colinboyd.co
Marie Forleo B-School marieforleo.com
Amy Porterfield Digital Course Academy
James Wedmore Business By Design
Denise Duffield-Thomas Money Bootcamp
Melissa Browne My Financial Adulting Plan
Jenna Kutcher jennakutcher.com

Some of my courses:
Site From Scratch
Limited Launch Formula
Fun With Funnels
Her Empire Builder

Let me know when your course is launching at:
hello@milliondollarmicrobusiness.com

index